The
Game
Changer

November, 2021

Charles,
To my friend + prayer partner.
Your gift of sharing your
heart through your writing
was an inspiration. Couldn't
have done this without your
example.

Kirk

The Game Changer

INSPIRATIONAL STORIES THAT CHANGED LIVES

Inspired and Compiled

by

IMAN AGHAY

Spotlight PUBLISHING

Goodyear, AZ

The Game Changer (Volume 6): Inspirational Stories That Changed Lives ©2021 by Success Road Enterprises. All rights reserved.

Print Book ISBN: 978-1-953806-69-7
eBook ISBN: 978-1-953806-70-3

Published by Success Road Enterprises | Spotlight Publishing™

Interior Design: Amit Dey
Published by: Spotlight Publishing™ - https://spotlightpublishing.pro

Ordering information: Copies of this book may be ordered directly from: www.mylifechangingmoment.com

TABLE OF CONTENTS

· · · ◆ ◆ ◆ · · ·

DEDICATION

·⸱✦⸱✦⸱·

To all the courageous
entrepreneurs serving the world
with their excellence and
leading the way for a better world.

INTRODUCTION

...◆...

I've been working with entrepreneurs and other successful professionals for the past sixteen years. As a business mentor, I see the complex interworking of an entrepreneur's life. I have the privilege of knowing what goes on behind the scenes. I am humbled when I see what it takes for entrepreneurs to realize their achievements.

The Game Changer Book Series is a collection of these behind-the-scenes stories – stories that most people never realize have laid the foundation for a successful business or company. These stories are personal, connected to the authors' hearts, and many of them are being shared for the first time with you, our reader. As I read this collection, I could not stop thinking about this old adage: *"Everyone you meet is fighting a battle you know nothing about! Be kind, always..."*

This book reveals some of the hardest times and darkest moments that entrepreneurs live through. Their experiences are real and deeply personal. Many of the chapters tell of bad choices and overcoming mistakes. However, all of them share something in common: a turning point—the turning point that changed the author's life forever. These stories are very dear to each author, and I am honored to be able to share their experiences with you. I hope that each of these stories touches you as deeply as I have been touched.

Iman Aghay

One Thousand Tiny Cuts Can Cause You to Bleed to Death

· · · ✦ ✦ ✦ · · ·

By Dr. Zynul D. Khan

"Hearing the opinion of people who knew practically nothing about me had a profound impact that made me feel even more worthless. Growing my opinion of myself out of what I know about me built my worth to recognize the positive impact I know I have on people today."

—Dr. Zynul D. Khan

ONE THOUSAND TINY CUTS CAN CAUSE YOU TO BLEED TO DEATH

· · · ✦ ✦ ✦ · ·

By Dr. Zynul D. Khan

My story begins today, in 2021, and although the events I describe were gradual over ten years, they overwhelmingly changed the trajectory of my life.

I am married, and my second daughter was born on the same day as my wedding anniversary at the end of December. It was amazing, as my wife gave birth at home. You see, I'm a doctor; hence birth is nothing new to me. The surreal moment was what happened after my gorgeous baby's birth. We were all lying on the couch, myself, my wife, my firstborn, and our newest addition, fast asleep, I might add, in front of the TV. Picture this in your mind, my wife just gave birth, and here we all are at home watching TV as if it was just a regular Saturday night. This moment was profound and one that is burnt into my memory forever. The highlight for the beginning of 2020, and we all know how that year went.

My slow spiral downward began after this extraordinary evening, and I had no clue about what was coming.

Let me tell you a little about myself. I have been a medical doctor for 15 years and have worked as a registrar – a middle management position in medicine – for the past 11 years. I have struggled to advance myself in medicine throughout my career, beginning with attaining my postgraduate qualifications in emergency medicine (EM). My high hopes of moving my career forward in EM faced a significant obstacle two years into the program when I wrote my first set of exams. To explain, I need to go back 20 years earlier when I was in medical (med) school writing my examinations. During my first experience with oral exams, I discovered I had a major psychological problem. They offer orals when needed to defend a pass, honors, or distinction, and I needed to prove I could pass the subject. The examiner asks questions like in a job interview, and for me, it was worse than job interviews. I had five orals in three days. It was brutal. I was the only one in my class who had to do this interview process five times. I failed them all and repeated the entire exam, which involved five challenging subjects six months later. Following my abysmal experience, I managed to get through those five subjects without having another oral exam.

When I made it to my final year in med school, low and behold, to my horror, they had recently implemented mandatory orals for all final exams. So now, I'm entering my final year exams with this massive psychological trauma, better known as Post Traumatic Stress Disorder or PTSD. Take a wild guess of what happens next. You guessed it, I failed.

In this medical school undergraduate exam system, you are allowed three attempts at any exam. I spent the next year slowly repeating these exams. The stakes were high. It was pass or go home with nothing after four years, and hundreds of thousands of dollars of school fees, food, and accommodation paid and nothing to show for it. Suffice it to say, I don't know how I did it. I remember when I was required to demonstrate one of the techniques used to examine the patient. Apparently, I had done a great job. At my oral exam, when one of the foreign examiners (they usually import a few external examiners to keep things fair) saw me entering, he said (and I paraphrase), "I remember you. You had an excellent bedside technique examining that patient."

He had been observing me, but I was so focused on the patient I blocked out everything that could distract me, a technique I used for public speaking. He couldn't and didn't know that this oral exam was my first of the second attempt, and that morning, his words gave me the boost of confidence I needed to get beyond the PTSD and pass it. It lasted into the afternoon for the next oral, again with a pass. However, the PTSD returned in full force for my final oral two days later, and I froze again. For my last attempt, I endeavored to learn every possible question they could ask in the oral exam. A lecturer told me that the examiners always stick to a finite number of questions for this subject and only asked more in-depth questions based on how well the student is doing. If they notice them struggling, they go back to easier questions. Why had nobody told me this inside tip for my first attempt? Finally, I managed to pass two subjects on the second attempt and the final oral exam on the last attempt. To my stupendous and surprised amazement, I became a doctor.

Now to my EM program's second-year exam. Here I am, facing another set of orals, and my brain freezes over. I can barely speak, and when I look at the three examiners in front of me, all I see is nothing: no empathy, no sympathy, no recognition, nothing. I sit there hoping for this torture to end, and finally, it does, after 20 minutes.

I possess this ability to never give up, which has been both a boon and bane. I have overcome many obstacles, and I also keep trying over and over. You know that saying, "the definition of madness is repeating the same thing over and over and expecting a different result"? That's me.

I digress. I failed the oral. I continued to fail, and the more I failed, the deeper into my hole of despair I fell, causing me to make horrible life decisions. For instance, at the age of 34, I felt I was getting too old and needed to marry. After four weeks of dating, I married the wrong woman, and we divorced a year and a half later.

I fail out of the program after three years. So now I'm divorced and a failure, the first time I had ever failed at anything, and it happened twice in the same year, in the two things that meant the world to me, being married and my career.

At this point, I am in burnout, and I can't see any other possibilities of what I can do. I am heading on a downward slide into depression. So, now I'm showing up for the paycheck at the hospital with no vested interest in improving myself, my work environment, or my health. I've stopped exercising, and I'm restless, staying out every night until 4 am, I'm not sleeping, and I'm spending everything I earn on useless things like expensive dinners and toys. In other words, I'm on the path to my destruction. I burnt myself out at 36 years old.

This physician burnout happens to many doctors and for much the same reason as it happened to me. It isn't a single event but a series of often insignificant events that gradually add up. It's like being in a lousy marriage and wondering when it all went wrong, with the most notable difference being that, as doctors, we feel we need to stay and keep helping others.

Institutions, bosses, and systems have a large part to play. Many mid-level and junior doctors feel that they can make no contributions, or if they try to contribute, it falls on deaf ears. While we joined this profession out of a profound sense of empathy, they beat it out of us before we left medical school. When we graduate, the system relentlessly begins to drown our creativity and our drive to achieve, eventually leaving us as hollow shells with the belief there is nothing left or nothing we can do.

I manage to shake off my despair with the help of a friend while traveling as the team doctor with another national sports team to Jamaica or Canada—I am not even connected enough to notice. She reminded me of our previous talks about pursuing a career in sports medicine. I wonder what happened to that dream. I immediately searched for programs and then switched to clinical and research-based degrees, eventually finding one I liked. I was accepted! I am ready to head back into the ring to fight again. Fast forward two years, and I'm graduating as a sports and exercise medicine doctor and scientist.

It's the beginning of 2020, and life is looking great. I'm married to the love of my life, and we've had our second child. What could go wrong? When February comes around, the department head calls me to his office, nothing unusual. However, when I arrive, it gets serious. He says I'm in trouble with the seniors of other specialties and, without any specifics, they want me removed. So, he offers me a lifeline.

At the time, I worked in an environment where management promoted colleagues based solely on education, not their experience. This situation frustrated me, making me feel worthless and unsuccessful. As a result, I no longer recognized myself as the person who had once had the dream of being a doctor.

As mentioned, I got a lifeline: a chance to manage the health and well-being of the staff. I embraced this post, as it was a glimmer of light that I had not seen in years. Although, since the position was new, they gave me no resources and expected me to do miracles. Using the resources available, I created programs to address the health and well-being issues of the staff. My new post ignited inspiration in me, and I felt alive again. However, it was not to last. One month later, my boss transferred to another hospital, and his replacement didn't possess the same vision of my potential. He began making mundane requests at first. Then the first blow came when he told me to man a new COVID area. I thought, no problem, they needed the help, and I would help. So, I got creative again and made a swab enclosure to protect myself and reduce the need for personal protection equipment. I managed this new assignment for a few months while still promoting wellness for the health of the staff.

The new year starts, and the new boss reassigns me to duties far below my qualifications. My supervisor is a junior doctor who recently graduated med school with no postgraduate qualifications. He is young enough to be my son. Usually, this change would not bother me, but it's been an entire year of growth and passion. I am devastated. Over the next few months, I am thrown into a tug of war of survival and proving my worth.

I mentioned earlier I have this innate ability: I never give up. When my boss offered me that olive branch, I started researching. My research led me to the world of business, and suddenly I realized I could be an entrepreneur. I became a voracious listener to podcasts, business books, and mentorship webinars, learning what they never taught me in medical school or any medically-based postgraduate program: business and how to run a business. I learned how to create a course and teach people with diabetes and obesity to control their blood sugar and achieve their healthiest weight. My life purpose is spreading my message of "there is a better way, and help is available." I am passionate about offering the lifestyle solution for lifestyle diseases to help ten thousand people with diabetes and ten thousand people with obesity to reclaim their lives.

My burnout has vanished. To my colleagues, I say, "Medicine is not the only thing that exists. The world is full of endless possibilities."

I dug my way out of depression and burnout by finding and embracing my passion. I found the light at the end of the tunnel by fighting hard when my bosses tried to shut me down. I have left that tunnel, and I am never going back.

By Dr. Zynul D. Khan

DR. ZYNUL D. KHAN

 Dr. Zynul Khan is a medical doctor with more than ten years of experience as a sports and emergency medicine physician. Graduating medical school was one of the most challenging and grueling experiences Zynul has had to endure. When he thought it was over, he encountered the pressures of specialty training.

As a result, Zynul's work and personal life went through a downward spiral, leading to burnout. Complete disengagement led to losing interest in his career until a friend helped reignite his spark of creativity and genius. He is now pursuing his second postgraduate degree in public health. Zynul has transferred his years of experience and training working with high-performance athletes and teams to managing diabetes and obesity. Using the techniques favored by athletes, he has built courses to help people with diabetes achieve blood sugar control with little to no medication, allowing them to live fulfilling lives. Zynul is also passionate about reversing the obesity pandemic plaguing our world by showing those affected and their families' effective ways of achieving their healthiest weight.

https://www.essentialacademy.org/dr-khan-page
linkedin.com/in/drzynuldkhan

Scan the Code with your smartphone
to view a message from Dr. Zynul D. Khan

Using Science to Engineer Communications So Analytical Thinkers Can Build Trust, Relationships, and a Better World

By Dr. Cat Shrier

"Science is a perspective. Science is the process that takes us from confusion to understanding in a manner that's precise, predictive and reliable – a transformation, for those lucky enough to experience it, that is empowering and emotional."

~ Brian Greene

"Oh Lord! Please don't let me be misunderstood!"

~ The Animals

CHAPTER 2

Using the Science of Psychology to Engineer Trust-Building Communications For People Who Are "Too Analytical"

· · ◆ ◆ ◆ ◆ · ·

By Dr. Cat Shrier

S itting in the front row of the auditorium, I reviewed my slides one last time, and then glanced over my shoulder as the crowd took their seats. The room rumbled with the low drone of an audience that was nearly all men - hydrogeologists and groundwater engineers here to learn from *ME* about the new findings of a National Academy of Sciences Study Report on a technology called "Aquifer Storage Recovery" or "ASR", which is where water is treated and placed down a well into a groundwater aquifer for storage and later withdrawal and use.

I had served for three years on that National Academies Study Committee - the youngest committee member by more than a decade and the only woman who was not an academic. I had already become one of the world's leading experts on the regulatory and other "non-technical" issues related to this technology (anything having to do with policy, planning, permitting, and public perception of ASR).

Since I held degrees in geology, civil and environmental engineering, I understood the more technical aspects of ASR, including the water quality and hydromechanical considerations. Unlike most of my technical colleagues, however, I had also worked in legislative offices, political campaigns, and regulatory agencies for years before changing careers. Consequently, most of my professional career had been spent working at the intersection between technology and policy.

In short, I had earned my spot on that stage.

I had my presentation down pat, having given it several times before. Once the National Academies study meetings were over and there were no more free trips for committee members, most of the other members had moved on to other projects. Consequently, the Committee Chair and I ended up pulling together most of the final report as well as this presentation on the findings. Since he was Chair of a university department, he asked me to represent our committee, which I had been doing for several months, presenting versions of these same slides several times to various organizations that had come to Capitol Hill and at conferences and workshops all over the United States and Canada.

But this was going to be my first time as a Keynote Speaker.

This was a fairly large event in Orange County, California, just outside of Los Angeles – an area where ASR had been an important part of their water management strategy for reuse and preventing seawater intrusion. There were a lot of powerful people in the audience who could really do a lot with the information I was providing. Having given this talk so many times before, I knew what to say, how and when. I had all my intonations and laugh lines practiced and polished. I had this talk down cold!

I wasn't nervous - I was excited, confident, and maybe even a little cocky.

As I was being introduced, I went to the side of the stage. I started doing exercises I had learned from a mentor I was working with on workshop facilitation, jumping and tapping my opposite knees to get my brain and body ready for this performance. I was fired up and ready to go!

Feeling the blood rushing through my veins, I energetically took the stage, bounding to the center and then stopping to face my audience. I smiled and scanned the room, taking in the energy from the 400 pairs of eyes all focused on me. I then walked over to the podium clicked on my first slide and started the show.

For 45 minutes, I spoke, filled with energy and enthusiasm for my topic and my message, connecting with my audience and ending with some important statements about the report findings and what they meant for the future of ASR!

As I finished, people applauded and began moving out of the room to get to the technical sessions. A few people came up to the stage to talk with me.

Then, I started to get the feedback.

"Loved your talk! Love your passion! Couldn't understand a word you said!"

UGH!

I tried hard to keep my smile and calm composure as my heart sank to my feet.

What did that mean, EXACTLY?

Did they mean they couldn't hear the sound system, or that I didn't speak into the mic? Had I been talking the whole time with bad sound while nobody said anything?

Was I using too many technical terms? I was used to talking to policymakers and community leaders, so I was typically careful to avoid both technical jargon and regulatory mumbo-jumbo.

Was I talking too fast or swallowing my words? That's something I've been known to do. In third grade, I had been diagnosed with "cluttering" (a speech defect) so I was normally very conscious of the need to *AR-TIC-U-LATE* my words.

Maybe my pitch was too high? I had heard that, when men get older and start to lose their hearing, they lose the ability to hear women's voices – or maybe that's an excuse they make up because they just don't think women have anything important to say?

I never did find out why my audience didn't understand me that day.

But then again, scientists, engineers, and other analytical thinkers are *not expected to communicate well*, and rarely are taught how to write and present in a way that is designed to accomplish our communications objectives.

As a water innovation expert, I had been working alongside leaders in water technology and public policy who were working to address such critical water challenges as climate change, aging infrastructure, and emerging contaminants. Communications challenges by Water Leaders were often cited as a major hurdle to gaining support for innovative and effective solutions.

That's why I created WaterCitizen initially – an organization intended to develop online media, education, and "WaterTainment™" that would enable Water Experts to use the internet to create courses and events; reach more people for less time, money, and effort; and more effectively build trust, build relationships, build collaboration, and build a better world.

I was completing a multimedia journalism program when I started WaterCitizen, but quickly realized that what I *really* needed to learn was online marketing and sales. I began studying with leaders in the education-based online entrepreneurship world where I discovered there were formulas and systems and blueprints and all sorts of scientific-sounding approaches available to craft better and more effective communications. Internet marketers LOVE data and can analyze what works and what doesn't in our marketing.

I developed programs to teach experts in water, the environment, and sustainability to educate, engage, and enroll more effectively online, drawing upon proven methods such as:

Iman Aghay's Ultimate Course Formula: conducting interview-based surveys and then designing and delivering beta programs with input from real students;

Jeff Walker's Product Launch Formula: a series of posts, downloads, videos, chats, and webinars used to enroll students based on Robert Cialdini's research published in the book *Influence*;

Virtual Event and Workshop Design based on the Experiential Learning Model; and

Justin Livingston and Callan Rush's Education-Based Marketing Methodology and Optimized Webinar Sequence.

In the years since I gave that keynote address, and especially since starting WaterCitizen, I have studied the ways in which scientists and engineers communicate and the attitudes about communications. The top three biggest communications challenges scientists and engineers face are as follows:

OUR ANALYTICAL NATURE: Analytical thinkers – those typically attracted to science and engineering and other analytical fields – experience the world differently and communicate those experiences differently internally (in our heads) and externally (in how we express ourselves). Neurolinguistic Programming or "NLP" is the study of how our brains (neuro) process experiences and turn them into language (linguistics). The "meta programming" for analytical thinkers tends to be as "mismatchers" (looking for what is different) vs "matchers (looking for commonalities). Roughly 75% of the world is matchers while only 25% are mismatchers.

Being a mismatcher is a gift, one that empowers us to identify problems, to analyze those problems and come up with creative solutions. If we grow up or work as adults in supportive environments where these gifts are appreciated, we can thrive. But if we're treated like there is something wrong with us because we think differently, those differences in how we think and express ourselves, which can be frustrating to matchers, may result in our being labeled as having "disorders."

Analytical thinkers may be discouraged from trying to communicate after being told over and over that we are too technical, too analytical, too confusing, or otherwise are just plain bad at communications. Particularly for men, they may be told to let someone else speak for them, playing into the absent-minded professor stereotype. For analytical women – who are expected to be naturally "better at communications" and "better with people" – we may face pressure to communicate and connect in ways that don't really come naturally to us.

OUR ANALYTICAL TRAINING: If we go into analytical fields such as science and engineering (as well as social sciences such as economics and policy analysis), we are trained to take a very dispassionate, objective, unemotional, and structured approach to collecting and analyzing data; formulating and testing ideas; and presenting our findings in a specific manner. We cannot use the same communications approaches we use with our professors and peers if we want to connect with other critical partners, stakeholders, policymakers, and clients.

OUR ANALYTICAL PROFESSIONS: As we move into our careers, scientists and engineers typically work in larger organizations, as documented in another National Academies study on scientists and engineers in the workforce. At work, we are further encouraged to "leave the communications and marketing to the communications and marketing teams" and just to stick to our analytical roles. Communications skills – outside of "technical communications" – are often devalued, marketing and sales are distrusted and characterized as "manipulation" by analytical types.

In some cases, we find even scientists and engineers who profit from keeping their work complex and confusing. For example, one of my doctoral committee members ran an in-house consulting practice at the university, winning large contracts where he had poorly paid grad students develop complex decision support systems based on numerical models. When he learned that I was creating knowledge-based decision support systems – which I developed from structured interviews with local experts and stakeholders, incorporating their input into my models, developing user-friendly graphical user interfaces and narrative results that real people could actually understand - he nearly blocked me from getting my degree, declaring my research to be "not real engineering."

Despite these barriers, is it possible for scientists and engineers to learn to communicate and connect better, sharing their expertise in a way that informs and inspires, educates, and engages, motivates and enrolls others into working with us in solving the world's greatest challenges? ABSOLUTELY YES!

As scientists and engineers – especially for those of us involved in public works, public health, and other forms of public service – it is so critical that we learn to "market" and "sell" our ideas. We already use a form of education-based marketing when we present at conferences. We need to understand what comes before and after those presentations and how to structure those presentations to produce specific results. We can use education-based marketing for funding or business development, to create collaborative partnerships or get support from decisionmakers, gaining "both buyers and buy-in."

Over the last 10 years, I've watched as crises like climate change and COVID escalate while scientists and engineers continue to struggle with communications, to be distrusted and accused to lying, and have our findings ignored. Using the science of human psychology and proven methods to engineer effective communications, analytical thinkers *can and must* learn share our knowledge and expertise, our research findings and our technologies in a way that can benefit humankind. WaterCitizen is here to help!

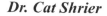

Dr. Cat Shrier

DR. CAT SHRIER

Working at the intersection of science and policy, engineering and communications, Dr. Cat Shrier has been an innovator in all things water. With degrees in Government, Geology, Environmental Management, Civil Engineering, and Multimedia Journalism, she knows her stuff!

Combining her background as a former Water Business Lead for a global consulting firm with experience in political & legislative campaigns and entrepreneurship, she has created programs that empower Water Leaders to apply online education-based business methods to gain "both buyers and buy-in." She founded WaterCitizen.Org in 2012 to support the Water Community in mastering virtual online approaches to building trust, building communities, building revenue, and building a better world!

Web: https://watercitizen.org
Facebook: https://www.facebook.com/cat.shrier/
LinkedIn: https://www.linkedin.com/in/catshrier/
Email: cat@watercitizen.org

Scan the Code with your smartphone
to view a message from Dr. Cat Shrier

Put One Foot in Front of the Other...

by Catherine Napoli-Cohen

"Don't let anyone tell you how to mourn, how to move forward, how to face tomorrow. Only you know what's best for you."

~ Catherine Napoli-Cohen

CHAPTER 3

PUT ONE FOOT IN FRONT OF THE OTHER...

· · · ✦ ✦ ✦ · ·

By Catherine Napoli-Cohen

S hit happens. There's even a t-shirt, so it must be true. Something does not go according to plan. We make plans – God laughs.

In so many ways, we remind ourselves that things don't always go the way we want them to. All too often, we simply accept the reality that things just happen. We settle for whatever comes, using "shit happens" as an excuse to avoid taking steps to move forward. Rather than push ahead, we incorporate the hurdle, adjusting to make it a new part of our lives and giving up whatever original plans we'd had. This new thing becomes our story, our identity, our life moving forward.

Shit happens, but it doesn't have to define us. Of course it changes us. Everything we experience, from the mundane to the extraordinary, changes us. The question remains, will we let this unexpected hurdle define us?

When I was 11 years old and my mother was 47, she became a widow. My father had a massive heart attack a few hours after we'd all returned from a family friend's 75th birthday party. Dad was a few months shy of 54 when he died. Crazy how the world works.

My mother chose to define her life as a widow. She never dated, didn't go out and find new friends, didn't create a life of her own. She simply told anyone who would listen that she was a widow. A sad, poor, lonely widow. When I got married many years later, Mom took every opportunity to let everyone involved know she was a widow. She had raised me by herself, was paying for the wedding all on her own, and was a widow.

Don't misunderstand – my mother was an amazing, wonderful, happy woman with children, grandchildren, nieces, nephews, siblings, and in-laws. She was truly a joyful person. Unless she wanted something. Then she pulled out the "poor widow" card and milked it for all it was worth. In those moments, I resented her.

On May 16, 2020, at the "ripe old age" of 55, I became a widow. Like my mother, it was fairly sudden, completely unexpected, and utterly devastating. My mother had died 7 years earlier, so she wasn't there to guide me or let me know what to expect from my new life.

My husband, Barry, and I had no children. We had moved away from our families in New York 25 years ago. Friends were the only family we had. Now my only family had left me. It was time to pick up the pieces and move forward. But how?

I decided a grief counselor was the way to go. Get everything out, look at it, resolve it. At our first session, I said something that perhaps shocked my counselor. Or at the very least, was unexpected. "Do not let me become my mother," I said. "She wore her widowhood like a badge of honor. Don't let me be her. I need to go forward. Whatever that looks like, I cannot live here, in this state of sorrow/sadness/grief/misery."

Over the next year, I learned a lot about myself: how strong I am, and about being at choice. I decided at the beginning of the next phase of my journey to move forward. Not move on. Moving on implies leaving something behind.

To choose to move forward, to put one foot in front of the other, is a deliberate step in healing. It isn't reserved for those who have lost a loved one. The choice to move on – or remain in place – is an option after any traumatic, life-changing event. It is the opportunity to allow ourselves to become whole again, even when that looks very different from who we were.

How, when, and why one decides to move forward is an incredibly personal matter. No one should tell you when the right time is. And yet, so many people will tell you what they perceive the right time frame to be for your personal process. No matter what you choose – and only you can choose – someone will find fault with your timing. It is far too soon, or already too late.

Moving forward, for me, is a choice I make every day. Some days, it is so easy to say, "Oh poor me. This is such a horrible thing that happened TO ME." It remains a conscious effort to not fall into that pattern.

The decision to move forward allowed me to decide which parts of the business Barry and I had run together I would take on as my business. Moving forward gave me the chance to discover who I was, just me. It let me fall in love with myself. The choice to move forward allowed me to begin a new relationship. I can be in love again without living in guilt. Guilt hits me sometimes, but I don't live there. Moving forward means I honor my past and love my future. Those most important in my life honor my past and look forward to my future, as well.

How does one move forward? By putting one foot in front of the other. It is a crawl, then a walk, and then a run. The first step is making the decision. Decide that moving forward is better than standing still or looking back. Yes, you will stand still sometimes and look backward a lot. But when you determine to move forward, you have a direction after your detour.

Don't listen to others, especially those who have never been through what you have experienced. Even those who share your journey live it differently. A few months after Barry died, my best friend from childhood tragically and unexpectedly lost her husband. Our situation is the same, but our journey is very different. We can support each other, tell our own stories, share the laughter and the tears. But each of us is very different. We suggest things we've tried that have worked, as well as the attempts that have failed. But we will never assume what is good for one is good for the other. The similarities of our situations and how we move forward end at "dead husband."

Your recovery and decision to move forward should be based on your timeline and no one else's. Some say God's time, not your time. God's time, Universe, Spirit, Whatever... it is all your time. My in-laws are amazing people. Supportive in the face of a tragedy no one should experience, the loss of a child. They told me they thought I should start dating, that it was time. And while that was a loving, strong, amazing thing to do, if the time hadn't been right for me, their blessing wouldn't have changed things. Move forward, or not, in your time.

You know you best. Listen to that small, still voice within. Meditate, pray, chant, scream. Do whatever it takes to hear the voices in your head and heart. They will guide you and carry you through your process.

Give yourself the gift of grace. Moving past the pain, the anguish, the impossibility of the situation takes everything you have. It calls for you to dig deep, to be raw, to be open. Some days you just don't want to get out of bed. Allow yourself the grace to feel, to rest, to scream, and cry. And then allow yourself the grace to move forward from wherever you are.

All we can do is take the next step. There is no crystal ball to tell us when the pain will subside. I can tell you it diminishes – or perhaps you just get used to it. But I can't tell you when or how.

Every minute of every day we are at choice. What do you choose? Life happens to us all. How you choose to move forward, or not, is entirely up to you. And most importantly, don't ever let anyone take being at choice away from you.

Catherine Napoli-Cohen

CATHERINE COHEN
CLIENT ATTRACTION EXPERT

Catherine is the co-founder of Cohen Coaching. A more creative force, Catherine is the ideas person. Ideas and inspiration seem to just come to her. Her specialty is taking a client's talent, experience, desire, and skills, and reworking them into new offerings, laying out the groundwork to get a new business started, or creating a path of growth and renewal.

Catherine enjoys crafting solutions that make sense to each client's unique situation. She is all about attracting the right clients to a business, so businesses grow organically.

She started life working in her parents' shoe store, taking care of customers, helping with inventory, and she even started networking as a teen. From being a lifeguard and swim instructor to being the software trainer to coaching, Catherine enjoys creating solutions. She is a natural born salesperson.

Catherine is also a Sci-Fi fan, (Star Wars more than Star trek) a Billy Joel fan (don't get her started) and attempted piano lessons in her youth. She also loves reading everything from Arthurian fiction to business books and a lot in between. She is not a fan of romance novels.

Even though she is a bigger Star Wars fan, Catherine had the United Federation of Planets logo put onto the train of her wedding dress in honor of her late husband.

FOR THE LOVE OF GREGORY

By Cheryl BryantBruce

"Every positive thought you have, every positive action you take creates a strong, positive energy that sends a ripple around the world, shifting the universe ever so slightly, making it a better place for every creature living in it. BE the light!"

~ Cheryl BryantBruce, M.D. (2002)

CHAPTER 4

FOR THE LOVE OF GREGORY

· · · ◆ ◆ ◆ · · ·

By Cheryl BryantBruce

Have you ever had someone crash into your world, changing the very fabric of your existence? On June 10, 1993, that day came for me when "Baby Gregory" burst forth into life. That day, I looked into the eyes of God and experienced pure love. Experiencing Gregory, I learned self-care, self-love, and to appreciate myself as my greatest asset. Maintaining health in all the facets of our lives allows us to live in dignity and grace, to fulfill our purpose of shifting the world in a positive direction. I became a light bearer. Sit with me for a while, and I'll tell you how and why I became a game-changer. Then, I will pass the torch to you.

Gregory was born at 2 pounds, 6 oz, 12 weeks premature. When my blood pressure elevated, it became apparent something was wrong. My beautiful pregnancy suddenly became a risk for my baby and me. I was emergently transferred from our Army hospital to an Air Force Medical Center. After a week lying in the dark to reduce stimulation, my kidneys shut down. My medical team immediately induced labor. A few hours later, the doctor called, "PUSH!" Both Gregory and his placenta torpedoed out.

Gregory is a beautiful baby with long hair standing straight on his head, a tiny, triangular, elfin face, delicate little lips, and huge kaleidoscope eyes that flash flecks of golden lightning, constantly changing colors. He reminds me of the cute little troll dolls popular in my youth. This tiny child seems to look right into your soul. The neonatologist observes, "He is an "F. L. K." (funny-looking kid). He looks syndromic to me." I don't find out which syndrome until nearly two years later.

The hospital couldn't diagnose Gregory's condition definitively, so we were transferred to a university teaching hospital nearer to home. The moment I arrived, although I attended an Ivy League medical school with a higher ranking than their own, if the medical team there acknowledged me as a doctor at all, they did so in a pejorative tone. They always incorrectly stated I attended a local medical school at a historically black college, never disguising they felt it and me inferior. They puckered on the title Doctor as if sucking on lemons. Their doctors and nursing staff rejected me as a colleague, uniquely qualified to partner in the care of my own child. After weeks of breastfeeding at the prior hospital, when I arrived at the university hospital carrying my stored breast milk, a young doctor dropped it in the trash in front of my face. I was told, "He'll get formula. Breast milk isn't good for preemies." I also carried a new, expensive bottle of liquid vitamin D. We already knew Gregory couldn't absorb fat-soluble vitamins A, D. E, and K due to his liver disorder. The doctor also dropped it in the trash, saying, "he won't need this either." Weeks later, Gregory had severe osteoporosis, and unable to clot blood, he began bleeding. Gregory weighed only three pounds, 11 ounces when he finally came home at age three months.

December 5, 1993, Gregory fell from the bed during a diaper change. He cried angrily but consoled easily, then fell asleep peacefully. In the morning, he did not look right. He looked exhausted and limp. He weakly lolled his head to the right. He cried shrilly, sounding like a cat. I rushed him to our army hospital. At six months of age, Gregory weighed only 6 pounds.

Upon arrival at the hospital, I asked the doctor to check for a closed head injury because of the fall from the night before. I was assured he appeared to be fine. He looked pale to me. His blood count was low. Once again, we went to the university hospital for further evaluation.

At the university hospital, Gregory's eyes rolled up and his breathing became shallow. He was still bleeding from morning blood draw sites. A scan of his head and eyes revealed more bleeding. An ophthalmologist unknowingly described a disease hallmark called posterior embryotoxin. Disregarding his medical condition, the hospital diagnosed child abuse/shaken baby syndrome. After weeks in the ICU in a medically induced coma, Gregory fought his way out of the coma and went to a regular ward.

The day before Christmas, social workers came to our door. In front of my other children, one handed us a court order, saying, "we are taking custody of Gregory. Merry Christmas." The other ran her finger over my freshly polished organ, looked at her co-worker and proclaimed that my home was more than adequate for "this type of people." I'll never forget the look of horror and bewilderment on my daughter's face.

We fought for months to regain custody of Gregory. We fought to gain proper treatment and to have Gregory receive compassionate care. All to no avail. Twelve months I watched my child dwindle, receiving inadequate care. It was Christmas again. I knew if I didn't do something drastic, I would never see another Christmas with my little boy. I searched the literature and came up with Alagille Syndrome, a rare liver disorder. The doctors refused to look at the literature, rejecting the possible diagnosis. I was desperate. While they continued to accuse us of child abuse, I knew that they ignored the underlying, unaddressed process that was continuing to ravage my child's little body. Finally, I took matters into my own hands.

With military precision, having mapped every detail to the second, on February 9, 1995, I stepped out on faith and kidnapped my own child. We crossed the state line headed for a well-known pediatric hospital. There, doctors expressed concern about the poor care he had received under the management of the other facility. He was close to death. A court order was obtained to hold him, so they could quickly diagnose and stabilize him. I was arrested at Gregory's bedside, charged with custodial interference, kidnapping, and interstate flight. I was labeled "Fugitive from justice." After the story hit the media, the judge released me on a signature bond, stating, "I hope my wife would have the courage to do what you did for the love of Gregory." They watched the news, so inmates and guards alike cheered my release. Sheriffs did a fundraising campaign to help with our legal fees.

Two days after Father's Day, following an emotional day in court, the judge reversed his own ruling. Baby Gregory was sent back to our custody to come home "to die." Baby Gregory was terminally ill, but I was determined my brave little son was coming home to live life fully. I fought for Gregory's life while he was away and would do so upon his return. When the going got tough, however, the "tough" walked away. My husband left me for his mistress, leaving me to solely care for our children.

Suddenly, I was a single parent in residency, working 36-hour shifts. Gregory required frequent extended hospitalizations. He and my other children had extreme post-traumatic stress, which caused severe separation anxiety. Each hospitalization brought fear that Gregory could be taken away again at any minute, even under our watchful eyes. I decided to homeschool for the well-being of all. Upon graduating from residency, I opened my own practice, which also housed our nonprofit for children with disabilities. My children attended school, worked, and played in the clinic. Initially, Gregory thrived, but as the clinic became busier, I spent less time with him directly. We put in long days. The children often ate dinner and fell asleep in the clinic. Gregory began to decline slowly. He desperately wanted and needed my constant attention, my constant loving touch reassuring him.

Gregory grew worse over the months. His doctors advised that I close my practice, sell my home, and go home to my parents to spend the last two months watching my son die. I closed the clinic, but I couldn't uproot my other children from our home. They had already sacrificed too much. I liquidated our savings, including their college accounts, for us all to live on. We went on welfare. We frequented food pantries to survive. Although I closed my clinic, I couldn't abandon the children the nonprofit served. I struck a deal with parents that when they needed me, I would make house calls. I suddenly became a much more effective physician. I saw my patients in their own element, understood their lives, their challenges. I became accomplished at motivating extremely positive change in their lives, helping them to become active partners in their own health care. I had developed a new health paradigm that would years later be coined "patient-centered care," emphasizing all aspects of health: emotional, mental, physical, financial, family, social, and spiritual. It is a wellness management model that worked for my patients, supported my own self-care and the care of my family. Gregory began to thrive again.

Fast forward a few months, and Gregory is doing so well that his gastroenterologist assured me he would live to be a teenager. This is a turning point in his disease process. We are ecstatic. We moved across the country for a fresh start, to California to be closer to my parents and for Gregory to attend a highly specialized school. Gregory continues to thrive. We all do. I find a new love interest. The kids find new friends. Gregory is growing stronger until suddenly, one day, his lab results show his liver is failing. Six months later, my beautiful angel dies at home in my arms. I watch the lights go out in his beautiful, kaleidoscope eyes, the gold flecks ceasing to flash. In the background, Gregory's favorite movie, "Lilo and Stitch," is playing. I hear Stitch telling Lilo, "Ohana means family. Family means nobody left behind." Our heartbeats had been synced for hours, but I no longer feel the flutter of Gregory's little heart. Except for the whooshing sound of his oxygen machine, there is complete silence.

Hours after Gregory died, standing in the rain as the hearse left with his body, I looked to the heavens and thanked God for the gift of my son.

Engulfed by a feeling of abject emptiness, the following day, I processed the thought that I could finally settle back into a regular practice. The word "settle" clanged loudly in my head. The alarms went off, "Don't settle for anything! Don't settle! Don't settle!" I had been given a gift, a new health paradigm. Now, it was my responsibility to use this gift to share my purpose, to teach the world a healthier, more fulfilling way of life. I was not yet ready. I plummeted headlong into grief.

I moved to Texas to escape my excruciating pain. There, I realized I couldn't outrun it. Fighting grief, I created one of the first concierge practices in the United States. Two years later, I moved to Beverly Hills, beginning a meteoric rise that landed me on a TIME Magazine 100 Most Influential People in the World list and in Town and Country Magazine as a top platinum concierge physician. I was on television, the radio, and spoke internationally. I gratefully acknowledge this notoriety was because one very special little boy taught me to live my life with grace, dignity, love, and gratitude. He taught me to savor each moment and live life to the fullest, always present in the moment. He helped me create a health-management paradigm, teaching the world how to live a sustainably healthy life with true abundance. In and through his kaleidoscope eyes, I saw the essence of pure love, for there, I looked into the eyes of God.

Life happens, but even amidst the severest of challenges, find the courage to savor the moments. You are your greatest asset. Appreciate that self-care, maintaining health in all the facets of your life allows you to live in dignity and grace, to fulfill your purpose of shifting the world in a positive direction. Live a life where love prevails. Gregory was a light bearer. He passed the light to me. I pass it to you. Game changing for the love of Gregory, BE the light!

CHERYL BRYANTBRUCE, M.D.

Cheryl BryantBruce, M.D., aka "The Celebrity Doc", has been recognized in Time Magazine's "100 Most Influential People in the World-for bringing back the "house call." She has been featured on CNN, NPR, Access Hollywood, and The Doctors.

Town and Country Magazine named her first of three top personal physician practices. In addition to being a busy physician entrepreneur, a gifted international speaker and author, Dr. Cheryl juggles a career in entertainment and has filmed on the sets of such epic films as Beverly Hills Chihuahua and Angels and Demons. Dr. BryantBruce specializes in Integrative Wellness Management and Longevity Medicine.

While Dr. Cheryl empowers all people to thrive in ultimate success and life fulfillment, using her "Windmill Paradigm," she especially guides purpose-driven leaders to reclaim your relationships, optimize your overall health and wellness, and manage your time. By leading you to fill your own cups, recognizing yourselves as your single greatest asset, she enables you to be enriched enough to embrace your purpose and empower others, filling your clients' cups as well. Two presidential administrations called upon her as an advisor. Dr. always strives to be a Master of Life and a world changer. The Doctor Is In!

Contact info:
Cheryl BryantBruce MD
9722 MacArthur Blvd. (Corporate Office) Oakland, CA 94605
DrCheryl@CherylBryantBruceMD.com
510-390-0335

LinkedIn: @CherylBryantBruceMD
Instagram: @CherylBryantBruceMD. @DrCherylMD
TikTok: @DrCherylMD
Twitter:@celebrity_doc
Https://CherylBryantBruceMD.com
https://thecelebritydoc.com

Scan the Code with your smartphone
to view a message from Cheryl BryantBruce

She's Having a Seizure

by
Denise Thomas

*"My dark days made me strong.
Or maybe I already was strong,
and they made me prove it."*

~ Emery Lord
When We Collided

CHAPTER 5

SHE'S HAVING A SEIZURE

· · · ◆ ◆ ◆ · ·

By Denise Thomas

Have you ever felt that something just wasn't right?
I was a new mom, and I had no clue what was coming. I had been very careful throughout the entire pregnancy.

This wasn't my first pregnancy. It had been a year since then. As the sun shone through the windows, I held my 4-month-old daughter as she was quieting down for a nap. It was strange to be thinking of that first pregnancy. So easy to conceive. So easy to lose when at 6 weeks pregnant I had awakened in a puddle of blood from a miscarriage.

Brandi was my first 'live birth.' It's a box I had to check on every doctor form. A painful reminder of the child I lost.

This pregnancy had been different. For 9 months, I hadn't lifted anything heavier than a gallon of milk. I hadn't edged the lawn or raked or mowed. I had been very, very careful, every day. And Brandi was a beautiful testament to our willingness to try again.

I was standing in our living room. The day was sunny and already warm. Brandi was dosing off in my arms and then . . .

My breath caught at the sight of my almost sleeping daughter. Her eye lids were slightly closed. Her little head was shaking back and forth. "Brandi? Honey, can you hear me?"

Nothing.

"Brandi?"... Please wake up... I could hardly breathe as I wondered what I'd done wrong to cause my daughter to be semi-conscious with her poor little head shaking back and forth, back and forth, and then it stopped.

It wasn't a long seizure, just a few seconds, but it seemed like an eternity. I silently prayed, "God help me! I don't know what to do!"

I told myself that it was just a passing thing. I was sure that I was wrong about what happened.

It was so short. I must have imagined it...

I didn't say anything to anyone, not even to my husband. I didn't want to be the overreactive mother.

I waited.

A few days later it happened again. This time a little longer. I was nursing her. She had come unlatched, and milk was running down her cheek. I prayed for answers.

I told my husband, but it was at least a week later before he witnessed it. She had had so many of these little seizures that I had lost count. We called her doctor.

My daughter continued to have small seizures, mostly occurring as she was nursing and almost asleep. Most of the time only her head or upper body was involved but sometimes it was her entire body. Those were longer in duration and much more terrifying.

At the doctor's appointment I explained what had been happening. There was no fever. No sign that anything was wrong. She was making strides in the typical infant markers, trying to crawl, trying to pull herself up along the furniture.

I'm fairly certain that the doctor was a little unsure of my description of events, or that perhaps they were imagined. She took notes but also took a 'wait and see' approach.

It wasn't until my daughter's 6-month appointment that the doctor witnessed a seizure. The doctor immediately made some calls, and we made an appointment to return the next day for an evaluation.

When we walked into the room, they were ready for us. They hooked my daughter's little head up to a multitude of wires while I nursed her to keep her still. I was nervous the entire time. She looked so little. Other than our anxiety, the tests were fairly painless and uneventful. We went home and waited for the results.

The doctor called a few days later and asked us to come back in. When we returned to the office the doctor suggested anti-epileptic drugs. The concern was that my daughter would fall while having a seizure and injure herself. Our home had hard floors and a fireplace with a large brick hearth. My husband and I just looked at each other. Together we said we would think about it and call her back with our decision in a few days.

Once home, we learned the possible effects anti-epileptic medications would have on our little girl. It would certainly slow down her progress. What was obvious was that the medication wouldn't actually fix the problem. The doctors didn't know what the problem was! All the medications would do is to cover up the symptom. We decided to forego medication and got busy padding and cushioning our home. We figured that would protect her for a few years anyway. We knew we might have to reassess later... but for now...

The seizures continued for many months. Sometimes they were short. Sometimes longer. Sometimes her entire body shook. All I could do was hold her. I told no one. I didn't want to talk about it. I had no answers. I just held her. Eventually, the seizures subsided and then ceased. For several months I waited, expecting them to return but they didn't.

I could finally breathe.

Five years later, at 2:36 am, I was rocking our infant son to sleep when, "Oh, God, no. No. Not again." Sean's head began shaking from side to side. Looking just like his sister had five years earlier. It was just as scary and the cause, just as unknown, but this time I knew, or hoped I knew, all would be well, eventually. I called his pediatrician's office to let them know what was happening and that we were making the same decision to treat our home with padding rather than our son with drugs. I just wanted it in his records. The doctor made notes. I prayed for strength.

This time, being a little more confident, I told my dad.

He said, "I am so sorry. That happened to your brother."

Wait, what?!

My brother, 14 years younger than me, had the same seizures after he was born. My dad said it occurred three times prior to mom leaving the hospital with him. Then it never happened again.

That news gave me a little solace and hope that whatever this is, doesn't appear to have a negative long-term outcome. My brother was an intelligent young man. He had graduated from a research university with high honors. So perhaps my children would be fine.

Every time my son had a seizure, I held him close and prayed, "God. Please let this pass."

After the first 12 or so seizures, I stopped counting. It didn't matter how many. By now I knew it would continue for some time.

And like his sister, eventually the seizures stopped.

··◆◆◆◆◆··

Sometimes we get an answer or a resolution to a situation that makes everything make sense. Sometimes we get a revelation that takes us from utter devastation to restoration.

Sometimes we don't. We don't always receive the answers we seek.

Sometimes the answer is simply to be strong for your children or your spouse.

I never thought I was strong enough until my daughter called. . .

"Mom. I think Ariel had a couple of seizures. I'm not sure if I imagined it because I'm looking for it, or if it really happened."

"I'm so sorry, honey." Together we both tried to be strong as we discussed what life might be like with my 5-month-old granddaughter having those same damn seizures that she had had.

How I wish my daughter didn't have to go through what I did. Decades later the fear still makes my heart quiver. My eyes still well up with tears at the thought of holding my daughter as her tiny body shook.

I prayed there would be more answers for my daughter than there had been for me thirty years ago. I researched the symptoms again. There had been only one study in the last 30 years. The conclusion wasn't reassuring.

A "rare seizure disorder" linked to a specific chromosome abnormality. Not useful. Most helpful was that 100% of patients with this type of seizure had one parent with similar seizures, and 66% had family members with a similar history. Unfortunately, the only remedy is still anti-epileptic drugs. There was nothing anywhere about a cure. But at least now we have a name for it and the prognosis was good.

I used to think, "Everything happens for a reason." And perhaps it does. However, what that reason is, is not always revealed.

Perhaps sometimes things happen so that, years later, we can help others get through a similar pain. Sometimes things happen to bring us closer to others and rely on their strength in our time of need.

We don't always get the answers we seek.

When you find yourself in a situation without answers, take a breath. Look around. There's always strength to lean on, sometimes that strength is inside of you.

DENISE THOMAS

TEDx speaker, international best-selling author, and coach to parents of college-bound teens, Denise Thomas inspires, educates, and equips parents to take an active role in supporting their children to live a life of financial freedom. Using her Cracking the Code to Free College strategy, her mission is to 'flip' the student debt statistic in the U.S.

Denise Thomas is a 20-year homeschool veteran having homeschooled her two children from Pre-k through high school. After a devastating bankruptcy and liquidation, Denise had to create a way for her two homeschooled children to pay for college and gain acceptance as homeschooled students. 7000 hours of research resulted in Denise's proprietary repeatable strategy and both of her teens attended their first-choice college on 17 scholarships exceeding $199,000, walking out of college with cash in hand. Denise says, you can keep your money. Send your kids to college on other people's cash!

"College doesn't have to be a Debt Sentence."™

~ Denise Thomas

Connect with Denise
Website: https://GetAheadOfTheClass.com
Blog: Parent Talk for the College Bound Teen -
https://www.getaheadoftheclass.com/blog
TEDx Talk- College Myths the Cost You Money:
https://www.youtube.com/watch?v=NDVpHZ7w1qA
Social Media & More: https://www.getaheadoftheclass.com/contact-me

Scan the Code with your smartphone
to view a message from Denise Thomas

HEALING AND SUCCESS THROUGH FAITH

By Dr. Jane Cheng

"Without faith, it is impossible to please God... we need to renew our minds daily, so we can create our life based on God's perfect will to create abundant life to be happy and wealthy."

~ The Holy Bible, Hebrew 11, and Romans 12

CHAPTER 6

HEALING AND SUCCESS THROUGH FAITH

···◆◆◆◆···

By Dr. Jane Cheng

Growing up, I was no stranger to abundance.

My father is a famous attorney and judge, and my mother is a schoolteacher. They are also entrepreneurs who have owned several businesses. They raised my brothers and me in an eight-figure-income home in Taiwan and invested heavily in our education and growth. In fact, I was the epitome of a well-rounded child: I took piano, dance, and art lessons and went to church regularly.

I was surrounded by family members who are doctors, attorneys, and successful entrepreneurs who gave their time and money to help the community.

Needless to say, I came to know abundance early in my life. My parents modeled an abundant mindset, so my brothers and I could see how to create lives we loved and use our success to help more people, too. They taught me that, if you listen to the voice of God and walk in His calling, He will bless you, and I saw examples of that truth everywhere I looked.

I experienced success early on as a child actress (imagine a Taiwanese Shirley Temple!) and went on to perform in television movies. I was a confident girl, participating in many school activities to learn to be a great leader and completing numerous public speeches and debates. Later, I embarked on my own entrepreneurial journey by starting a school for actors.

Eventually, because I'd learned the value of a great education, I came to the United States for graduate school.

And that's when things changed; I found myself facing language and other culture-related challenges.

I couldn't quite understand my professors; English is my second language, but they spoke so fast and covered so much material in each class!

I was overwhelmed, and for the first time, I experienced what it's like when limiting beliefs get in the way and keep you from achieving what you want.

It was *hard*. I was so stressed, I even started to feel hopeless… which wasn't like me! I questioned my ability to complete graduate school (I call this the "I can't do it" mindset/limiting belief).

**That's when my parents suggested something critical
in creating an abundant and happy life: seeking help.**

They encouraged me to find a church community. I did, and through the Bible's teachings, I learned to trust God… to have faith that He rewards those who seek Him. Even now, I return to the Bible verse that says, *"Be transformed by the renewing of your mind. Then, you will be able to test and approve what God's will is – His good, pleasing, and perfect will."*

Because I know guidance and mentorship are invaluable, I also simultaneously sought counseling, where I learned to take smaller steps: to plan and to take action, one step at a time.

**Most importantly, I learned that you *must* receive healing
to overcome your limiting beliefs.**

Eventually, I received that healing, and my faith and mentorship guided me through not only overcoming the limiting beliefs that were keeping me stuck, but through the completion of four master's degrees and two doctorate degrees. Why? Because I was healing holistically –emotionally, physically, spiritually, and financially – and *that* is the key to abundance.

Throughout these years of schooling, I took several jobs to help pay for my tuition. I worked in hospitals, clinics, and communities as a healthcare worker and as a chaplain and therapist. I've served as a pastor in more than seven American churches, for congregations ranging from 100 to 10,000 members.

My goal: to help people heal holistically –
their physical body, mind, and soul –
to find their life purpose and live an abundant life.

But my battle with limiting beliefs wasn't over yet.

During and after my advanced schooling, **I strongly believed I needed to give away my services, or offer them at a very low cost, to make them more accessible to more people** (recall the strong values my parents instilled in me around success being a vehicle for helping people).

In and of itself, that limiting belief stopped me from earning a healthy income. But it was compounded by yet another: **that I wasn't good enough to charge higher fees, anyway.**

For the first time in my life, these beliefs culminated in low self-worth and depression. That, in turn, resulted in anger. For so long, I worked jobs I didn't like, but was good at. I made decent money in healthcare but didn't love what I was doing. And then, when I *was* doing what I loved – ministering – I wasn't making good money!

The bills piled up; at one point, I had $100,000 in credit card debt. I was *so* worried about my finances yet felt incapable of changing the situation. If I couldn't even pay my bills, how could I help others?

And if I couldn't get paid to help people, how would I ever pay my bills? It was a vicious cycle, and I found myself wondering whether "this" was all there was to life.

Again, I sought therapy and turned to my faith.

Therapy helped me remove my limiting beliefs around giving away my services. I worked through each of them, constantly reminding myself that my services are backed by more than $1 million and 35 years invested – not only in education in medicine, divinity, psychology, and business, but in coaching and mentoring. *Of course,* I could charge higher fees that reflected the value of my service and the fact that I'm a unique leader who has served thousands of clients and impacted so many families with holistic healing!

Church reminded me of my inherent value as God's creation, and that I have special gifts and talents I can use to help others. I found comfort in the Bible: "Without faith, it is impossible to please God. We must believe He exists, and He rewards those who earnestly seek him."

I resolved my faith, knowing He will reward me with financial blessings from people who are willing to pay for my service – my tribe.

I found the answer to the question, "Can I create work I not only love, but am *passionate* about… AND make good money doing it?"

YES!

Through my business, Care and Counseling Coach Center, I combine psychotherapy with spiritual and life/business coaching to offer holistic healing, not only guiding my clients to live an abundant life, but to *ignite their fire* to live their most fulfilled, passionate, and joyful lives!

And I'm living **my mission: to empower entrepreneurs to have the courage and boldness to play big – to step into their vision and dreams – by creating a business aligned with their soul's purpose.**

Through all I do, I return regularly to the following tenets:

1. I trust God in faith to receive healing and be whole.

2. I allow God to renew my mind, to heal my limiting beliefs, and to attract my tribe: those people who want to work with healing and mindset.

I now know that *because there is a body-mind-soul connection, you MUST change your mindset to change your business.* This is what I teach my clients: I help them reclaim their destiny, own their personal power, and create unlimited success.

I am proud of who I am and what I'm called to do as a spiritual advisor who brings healing and hope to so many. As a wealth mentor, I empower people to double and triple their income and elevate their energy. And as a success coach, I guide people to remove their mental blocks and change their limiting beliefs, resulting in unprecedented happiness and wealth.

It's my *passion* to empower people like you to live an abundant life – and that includes making six figures! One of my core principles is that, when you align your business with your gift, you attract clients more than willing to pay for your services. And you make the impact and create the change you want while enjoying a profitable business!

You don't have to take my word for it! Here are some results my clients have seen during our work together:

- *TK was able to regain confidence and clarify her message, which resulted in the sale of several $5000 packages as she turned her business into a vehicle for her mission to impact many people.*

- *CR was able to attract more clients and double her fees! She continues to remove limited money blocks to attract more money miracles.*

- *SF was able to receive holistic healing to remove trauma emotions from her past. Doing so allowed her to transform her business, serve many in the community, and double her income and impact.*

- *JM was able to find his true identity and calling in life. With increased confidence, he raised his high-end package fee to $8,000.*
- *CH was able to grow her business and confidence so much, she increased both her client load and income by five times!*

Now, to give you an example of the work we can do together, I'd like to share with you my Bold Money Process, which I designed to empower you to have an abundant money mindset, so you can make a bigger impact – and of course, more money!

BOLD MONEY: Be BOLD to Focus on Your Brilliance

B: Be bold! Don't play small. Play big to focus on creating your best life, based on your calling and purpose. Focus on your unique gifts and brilliance to create a business and a life you love! You'll be the best version of yourself, and you'll truly enjoy your life.

O: Open your mind. Allow the Universe or your higher power to guide your intuition, which will choose the right path for you. When you tune in and listen to your higher power, you'll be rewarded, financially.

L: Love what you do – do what you love. Find out who you were born to be and what you were born to do, so you can love what you do daily – and create a business around it. When you do, you'll make more money and enjoy the most abundant life!

Not sure where to start?

Spend time meditating. Write down who you really want to be as your true identify, outside of anyone else's expectations. Explore your passions – what kind of work do you really enjoy and feel called to do? Answering these questions will lead you to the business you are called to do on this planet.

D: Claim your destiny. Step into your power. Be clear about the legacy you want to leave. When you are clear about your destiny and future dream, you can regain confidence and power from the universe. You'll have what you need to step out of mediocrity and create an abundant life you love!

M: Develop a healthy money mindset. Identify and change negative money mindsets that hinder your ability to receive financial blessings from your tribe. When we charge our worth, our clients pay us to support our own visions as they make a commitment to their own work toward transformation. The result: We continue growing our own vision to double our impact and income without feeling guilty about charging our worth as we build up a loving community! If we don't charge an amount commensurate with the value of our service, we are limited as to how many people we can serve.

O: Open yourself to have fun and enjoy life! Leverage your working time, so you have more time freedom (consider offering group coaching or one-to-many packages). Plan for time with your loved ones and pets. This will bring you positive energy and elevate your vibration … and you'll attract more fun, clients, and money!

N: Say "no" to distractions. Focus on one main thing; take back your time and build your business and life according to your new identity and new calling. Let go of those things that don't bring you closer to living your vision, and step into your leadership as an entrepreneur who is changing the world.

E: Evaluate how you spend your time, money, and energy. Change your habits accordingly. Spend as little time as possible with people who make negative comments or talk down to you. They rob your confidence and power! And stop doing tasks that steal your energy (delegate them if you can't forego them all together). Invest in your personal growth and become empowered to transform your money mindset.

Y: Say "yes" to opportunities to grow yourself and your business. It's *so* important to invest time, money, and energy into personal growth classes. These classes help you change your mindset, habits, and behavior, so you can have better relationships with yourself and others while you grow spiritually, emotionally, and financially. Also, the more you focus on growth, the more you'll grow! Seize the opportunity when the universe sends you mentors.

No matter what the past holds, each of us has experienced some kind of trauma that created limiting beliefs. I'm a perfect example. I had a wonderful childhood! I was surrounded by loving, generous family members who had an abundant mindset and wanted to help others. They gave me everything I needed to be successful and happy.

Yet the limiting beliefs hindered me all the same. When I began experiencing some that kept me from the abundant life I deserved AND the impact I longed to make, it was only through faith, mentorship, and personal growth that I learned to transform them.

I believe in you! You, too, can overcome any limiting beliefs you have and become an even better version of yourself! You, too, can find a tribe that is willing to pay you for your God-given gifts and talents. And you, too, can create an abundant life you love… one that gives you great joy and the opportunity to change lives!

Get Dr. Jane's gift, **The Healthy Money Relationship Quiz**, to identify and repair limiting beliefs in your relationship with money, here:

https://liveyourbestpurpose.com/how-healthy-is-your-relationship-with-money/

DR. JANE CHENG

Dr. Jane Cheng is a gifted healer, spiritual mentor, wellness advisor, and success coach who helps people create their businesses around work they LOVE by using their unique gifts, which allows them to align with their soul's purpose and transform lives.

She has invested more than a million dollars in personal growth and professional education and earned four master's degrees and two PhDs in medicine, divinity, psychology, and business. In addition to her work as a coach, Dr. Jane has worked as an ordained pastor. She integrates all her knowledge and life experience to bring holistic healing – emotional, physical, spiritual, and financial – to her clients and to coach people to double their income while living their soul's purpose.

You can learn more about her here:
http://www.liveyourbestpurpose.com
https://decaturpsychotherapist.com.

Scan the Code with your smartphone
to view a message from Dr. Jane Cheng

I Thought I Was a Worthless Piece of Trash

By Janelle Anderson

To be yourself in a world that is constantly trying to make you something else is the greatest accomplishment.

~ Ralph Waldo Emerson

CHAPTER 7

I Thought I Was a Worthless Piece of Trash

· · ◆ ◆ ◆ · ·

By Janelle Anderson

When I was sixteen, my boyfriend died. My heart broke into a million pieces. I didn't know how to process the grief. I filled the void with food and numbed the ache with marijuana. By the time I started college, I was thirty pounds heavier. I felt unattractive, unlovable, and alone.

One night during my sophomore year, my roommate and I went out for some fun. We played foosball and talked to cute guys. We were having a great time. I recognized one of the guys as my secret crush. I had seen him around campus. Everything after that was a blank until I woke up in my bed with a man on top of me – my secret crush. I couldn't figure out what was happening. I couldn't move or speak. Everything went black again. I woke up and saw blood on the sheets. With a sickening wave of realization, I thought, "Oh no! I lost my virginity in a one-night stand with some guy I don't even know! I must be a worthless piece of trash."

I began a desperate search for love – to feel worthy of love. I literally looked for love in all the wrong places. As I went from one man's bed to the next, I only felt more worthless. I was passed around the football team and contracted a venereal disease. I endured an unwanted abortion. I almost flunked out of college.

One afternoon, at the age of twenty-three, I sat on a barstool in a Las Vegas casino. My stomach churned. My heart pounded. I wanted to run, but my boyfriend stood at the exit door, watching me. I felt trapped. Nowhere to run. Nowhere to hide. Nowhere to turn for help. A man sat next to me smelling of booze and cigarettes. He turned to me and asked, "Are you working?"

My heart and mind screamed, "No!" but I said, "Yes." We went to his hotel room. He paid me. I sold my body, but it felt like I sold my soul. This scene played out day after day, month after month, year after year – hundreds of times over the next three years. By the time I was twenty-six, I was a hardened shell of a woman. I hated myself for what I had become. It was all my fault. I was a worthless piece of trash.

One night, my boyfriend and I had a terrible fight. On the floor, pinned under him, with his hands around my neck choking me, I thought I was going to die. Suddenly, he came to himself, released me, and fled the apartment. Panic-stricken, I reached for the phone to call my mom, sobbing uncontrollably. It was the middle of the night, but thankfully, she answered. I'll never forget what she said to me: "Jesus wants you to come home to him. He wants you to have peace."

I prayed with my mom. When I hung up the phone, I experienced a powerful presence of peace that filled my being from head to toe. Something changed. Suddenly I was no longer afraid of what my boyfriend might say or do. He tried intimidation, threats, mind games, and lies. He told me he had lost all our money gambling, so I would have to go back out on the streets. He shamed me for accepting money from my parents. But nothing worked. I was no longer trapped. I was set free by the mighty power of God's love.

I moved from Vegas to Virginia, but I dared not tell anyone for fear that they would reject me. My shame silenced me. A year later, I married the man who had trafficked me. Who else would want to marry me? He knew my past. Inside I was still a worthless piece of trash.

For the next six years, I lived in two worlds. One world seemed to make sense according to my husband. The other, when he was not around, looked so different and normal. My life was full of turmoil and confusion. Everything wrong with our marriage was my fault. Something was wrong with me; that was what he told me, and I believed him. Then one night he packed up his things and left without a word. By this time, we had a three-year-old daughter.

I moved home to Virginia. My husband and I divorced, and I was finally free from that relationship. I began my teaching career, which had been my childhood dream. My daughter flourished, I married a man who truly loved me, and we settled into a good life. But something was not right. The secrets of my past haunted me and silenced my voice. I could not be authentic. I could not be vulnerable. I armored up and hid behind a wall. I was disconnected from my true self and lived in a world of pretend, trying to be whomever I needed to be to fit in and be accepted.

In my mid-fifties, I hit a wall. There had to be more than what I was experiencing, but I felt stuck. Over the years, I have had many conversations with God. I see pictures in my mind, scenes that unfold before me. He speaks to my heart through them. During this time, I saw a walled garden. Inside the wall, everything was lush, green, and full of fruit. Beyond the cultivated portion, I noticed weeds and thorns and twisted, barren plants. Jesus walked to that area, picked up a gardening tool, and looked at me with a question in his eyes.

The message was clear. If I truly wanted to tear down the wall and move forward, I needed to face my past. With the help of counselors and people who loved me, I dug deep in the garden to clear out the weeds. I discovered the story I had been telling myself was not true. I was never a worthless piece of trash. I had not "lost my virginity in a one-night stand." The truth was I had been drugged and raped. I did not choose a life of prostitution. The truth was I had been trafficked.

What happened to me was not because I was worthless. It was because men chose to take advantage of a vulnerable young woman. Like many women who have survived sexual assault, I believed it was my fault. The truth was I had been traumatized and abused. As I finally accepted the reality of all that had happened, the weight of shame lifted from my soul. I embraced my value. I embraced my worth. I embraced the truth that I have always been worthy of love.

Since then, I've dedicated my life to helping women discover their value and worth. So, now I have two questions for you: Do you know who you truly are? What secrets are hidden in your soul? Perhaps you grew up in a home full of addiction and got caught in its grasp. Maybe you were bullied as a child or struggled with learning difficulties. You may have been told you're no good, or you don't belong, or you'll never be successful. Perhaps you were sexually abused and blamed yourself. Whatever your secret struggles may be, you can find your truth, just like I did.

Through my journey, I've identified four distinct stages of healing. I share them with you in the hope that you will find them helpful. I call this the STAR Process because I found that I transformed from a "worthless piece of trash" to a fearlessly confident woman who became a star – the star of her own life.

The first stage is the "stirring of the soul." This happened when I became aware of feeling stuck. Alarm bells woke me to the fact that life was passing by quickly, and it was time to act. The emotional ties with the past can be difficult to cut, and you may feel resistant to change. I was comfortable in that outer garden, and the thought of cutting into the weeds of my past was not pleasant. In fact, I resisted for an entire year after I saw the garden vision. But the stirring in my soul was stronger than the resistance. When you feel that stirring, that something needs to change, lean into it. The resistance you feel is normal. When a mother eagle knows it's time for her babies to leave the nest, she will stir it up so that it becomes uncomfortable. This forces the eaglets to try out their new wings.

There is a transition period when the eaglets resist and try to stay in the nest. Finally, though, they spread their wings and fly. This is what this stage can feel like. You know that greater things are ahead for you. The unknown can be scary and exciting at the same time. As you lean into the energy of this stirring in your soul, it becomes easier to let go of your old ways of being and thinking and step into the new season.

The next stage is "telling the truth." This is usually the hardest part, but it is essential. You must take an honest look at what you believe about yourself. Embedded lies come to the surface so you can see them for what they are. The lie that I was a worthless piece of trash had driven my life in many ways, but I couldn't see it. When exposed to the light of truth, it lost its power. This is an excavation of the soul, but it's worth the work to get to the truth. Tell yourself the truth. Be real and transparent. It may hurt at first, but soon you'll find sweet release as you let go of who you thought you were and embrace who you truly are.

The third stage is "acceptance and activation." This naturally happens because when you know the truth about who you are, acceptance is easy. You see the beauty of your unique design, your strengths, and your gifts – who you were always meant to be. I recognized my natural ability to draw out the best in people and my love of speaking and teaching. My voice was no longer silenced as I stepped onto many stages to share my story. I was no longer stuck. Activation happens in this stage because you are free from the false identities that once weighed you down.

The final stage is a full "release of the river" inside. There is a flow and ease to your life when your past no longer holds you back. The river inside you is the essence of your true self – who you were designed to be. You no longer strive to be someone else. You become yourself. You become the star of your own story. You embrace your worth and value. You impact the world and change the environment around you – just by being you.

Life is too short to spend it being someone you're not. No matter how dark your secrets seem to be, they only have the power you give them. Bring them out into the light of truth and watch them crumble like dust in the wind. The truth is you are a person of great value and worth with a destiny to fulfill. Don't let anything hold you back from stepping into the power of that truth. Become who you truly are. It is the greatest accomplishment of all.

Janelle Anderson

JANELLE ANDERSON

Janelle Anderson is a speaker, author, and coach specializing in helping women entrepreneurs discover their inner confidence superpowers. Her passion is to help women know their immense value so they will show up, stand up, and speak up in fearless confidence. As a survivor of sexual abuse, Janelle once believed that her voice didn't matter. In her mid-fifties, she experienced deep inner healing and was able to break off the shame of her past. She discovered the power of knowing who she truly is and began sharing her story to empower other women to do the same.

At age sixty-one, Janelle earned her coaching certification from the Institute for Professional Excellence in Coaching and started her business, Emerging Life Coaching. Her signature program, Fearless Confidence Formula, guides women through a step-by-step process to discover their unique message and to speak up with confidence so they can impact the world through their business.

Janelle's first book, *Come into My Garden*, is available on Amazon. Her new book, *Take Center Stage: Be the Star of Your Own Story*, is due to be released by the end of 2021.

Connect with Janelle

Email: janelle@emerginglifecoaching.com
Web: www.emerginglifecoaching.com/
Facebook: www.facebook.com/emerginglifecoaching/
LinkedIn: www.linkedin.com/in/emerginglifecoaching/

Scan the Code with your smartphone
to view a message from Janelle Anderson

I AM...

By Jenn Eastwood

"Our lives change externally as we change internally."

~ Caroline Myss

CHAPTER 8

I AM...

· · + + ◆ + + · ·

By Jenn Eastwood

I AM – two of the most powerful words for what you put after them shapes your reality. – Lee Bevan

THAT is a lesson I learned in a profoundly painful way.

For the majority of my life, the words I put after I AM were repeated so many times in my mind that they became my reality. Those words were: I AM flawed, I AM inadequate, I AM a disappointment. Though I wasn't aware of the words, I was keenly aware of the feelings these words created: shame and discomfort.

So, I hid the deepest parts of me, not only from others, but also from myself. I accomplished this by excelling at everything. I was a "good" girl, worked hard, and achieved. Perfection was my goal so people would not see my self-perceived inadequacies. I pushed myself to be the perfect daughter, the perfect employee, the perfect spouse, the perfect mom, the perfect person. My "perfect" persona was so ingrained, I was not aware of what I was doing.

My approach worked well for quite some time. I was an A student, bought a house, got married and had two kids before 30, became an audit partner in a regional accounting firm at 35, all while building a fun social life. To other people I had it all. I even convinced myself that I had it all. My life fit together perfectly. Yet, there was discontent brewing internally because my external reality conflicted with my internal reality. My underlying thought was if people really knew me, they would conclude that I didn't deserve success. I added the following words after I AM: unworthy, a fraud, an imposter. So, I worked harder and harder to maintain my standard of perfection (meaning never make a mistake, never fail, never struggle, do it all – flawlessly). I took people pleaser and overachiever to an extreme.

What I didn't realize was that each piece of my "perfect" life was delicately put together, ready to fall like a house of cards. My strategies to maintain my "perfect" life created a constant state of internal stress and anxiety. My "perfect" life was unsustainable. The pieces of my "perfect" life slowly crumbled as I struggled through my first year as an audit partner and collapsed when I discovered my husband's (now ex) affair.

As my marriage fell apart and I stepped down from the partnership, I added another word after I AM – a failure. These "failures" knocked me down, disoriented me, and left me questioning how to get back my "perfect" life. I was filled with shame. And now there was evidence of my inadequacies. To protect myself, I added another word after I AM – innocent. If my ex had been faithful, I would still be married and an audit partner. My life would still be "perfect." I was unable to face how I had contributed to the collapse.

I frantically tried to put the pieces of my "perfect" life back together. However, the pieces no longer fit. Then I met Mark. He adored me and made me feel special, despite my flaws and my "failures." A new word began to emerge after I AM – loved. It felt amazing, and I didn't want the feeling to go away. So, I rebuilt my life with Mark. We got married and had a baby.

Our "perfect" life hit major bumps when Mark lost his job, required major back surgery, and was in two motorcycle accidents. Each of these events were hard on both of us. However, Mark also struggled with depression, which put an additional strain on our relationship. I tried to convince myself that I had put all of the pieces back "perfectly," and my life was whole again. Yet, deep down, I knew that the pieces still did not fit together quite right. I did not want to face the discontentment and unhappiness that I began to feel. Instead, I focused on my marriage commitment, determined to make it work. I fell back into people pleaser and overachiever mode.

The unhappiness and discontentment I felt with my personal life began to extend to my professional life. As the unhappiness and discontentment grew, the pieces of my life that were barely in place started crumbling. The thought I AM loved was replaced by my original thoughts: I AM flawed, I AM inadequate, I AM a disappointment. I began taking on more and more, until my body forced me to stop with severe back and hip pain, leading to three major surgeries in less than a year. I added new words after I AM – helpless, defeated, a victim. Fueled by anger and resentment, I found myself showing up in ways that I did not like. I no longer knew who I was or what I wanted. I only knew that my life was not working. Something needed to change.

I began trying to figure out what I wanted and how best to fit the pieces together to create a life that worked for me. I read many books, worked with different life coaches, and participated in personal development events and courses, which helped me understand that each piece of my life was built on a shaky foundation based on feelings of inadequacy. I began creating a new and more solid foundation based on self-love and self-acceptance. However, my new foundation was not fully developed and was easily shaken.

I began making sense of what was going on with my marriage. Mark was struggling with mental health issues. Because of this, there were two distinct sides of him. There was one side of him that was the loving, kind, and wonderful man I married, which reinforced my belief that I AM loved. The second side of him was angry, impulsive, and mean. This side reinforced my beliefs that I AM inadequate, a failure, innocent. The more Mark's second side came out, the more my I AM inadequate, a failure, innocent, came out, which only trigged

Mark's second side to appear more frequently. We were in a vicious cycle that we needed to break.

With all of the self-acceptance work I was doing, new thoughts emerged – I *can* learn. I *can* make my life better. Now I had a new word after I AM – responsible! With this word came power; power to focus on me and how I was showing up. As I discovered strategies and resources that supported me, more new words emerged: I AM — strong, resilient, capable, resourceful! Each time my unstable foundation was shaken, and I was knocked off, I dug deep and focused on learning from the situation. Instead of saying I AM a failure, I started saying I AM learning. This helped me get up, brush myself off and climb back on. Each time this happened, my foundation was becoming a little stronger, a little more stable. It took more to shake it. And when I was knocked off, it became easier and easier to get myself back up.

Yet, things with Mark continued to be rocky. Mark knew his actions hurt me, and he didn't want to do that. In February 2019, we decided to separate. We hoped we could work through things and come back together. However, shortly after moving out, Mark gave up hope that therapy was going to save our relationship and our family. Although he loved us and wanted to be with us, he knew that he would need to face his demons, demons that he believed were impossible to face and overcome. My hope that we could work things out was crushed, and our conversations turned towards divorce. The pieces of my life were shifting and rearranging in a painful way. Yet we both believed divorce was the best for all of us. What I didn't realize at the time was this was just the beginning of the most painful events of my life.

Shortly thereafter, Mark became impulsive. His actions did not make sense and were totally out of character. Mark's actions shook my foundation and I struggled to not sink with him. And then, on July 24, 2019, I received a call that Mark had shot himself in the head. Mark was dead. There was no warning, no note, no explanation. My foundation collapsed, burying me. In that instant all of the pieces I had been rebuilding were shattered; my life was forever changed.

Nothing felt right or made sense. The word that formed after I AM – lost. I was paralyzed. My future triggered extreme anxiety, so I started focusing on getting through one day at a time. When the pain felt unbearable, I focused on getting through one breath at a time. I gave myself permission to not be okay in that moment. At the same time, I held onto my faith that eventually I would be okay. My mantra became: I can get through this, I AM stronger than I think I am, I AM brave, I AM capable, I AM resilient.

Initially, these I AM beliefs were hard to hold onto. However, as the days went by, my mantra became more ingrained, I became stronger, and my foundation became more stable. I began focusing on healing and making peace with what happened. I knew Mark loved me and our family deeply. He also had told me that he felt like a burden to us. This led to the thought: Mark loved us so much that he was willing to die to set us free. In his eyes, he was giving us a gift, the gift of freedom.

Yet there was doubt. Was I really worth Mark dying for? Initially, my answer was a strong no, as I blamed myself for not knowing and doing more. Yet, I knew that this was not honoring Mark. And I wanted to honor him by accepting his final gift. I began working on forgiving myself and him. The more work I did, the more I healed, and the more love I felt. This led me to replacing I AM lost with I AM loved. This love was stronger than any love I had ever experienced as the love was internal, not external. This allowed me to accept Mark, his decision, myself, and our story.

I continued to focus on all the gifts that I received from Mark. He truly was my soulmate. Mark taught me many lessons about myself, love, relationships, and life. He challenged me to expand, grow, and become a better version of myself. His impact will be with me forever because he helped me find my way home – home to myself.

Being home within myself is about loving and accepting myself, flaws and all. This has created a new understanding of perfection. My flaws aren't something to hide or overcome. They make me who I am.

And I am "perfect" just as I am, not despite my flaws but because of my flaws. This change in my understanding of perfection was the piece missing from my life. It is what creates an unshakable foundation and the glue that holds all of the pieces of my life together. The more at home I feel, the easier it is to trust my intuition and show up as I AM. The more I feel at home, the more powerful I feel and the less I look to the outside for love and validation. My love and validation come from within. No matter what happens externally, I AM whole, I AM complete, I AM connected, and as a result, anything is possible. Now I am in a place in my life that I never thought possible – I AM comfortable in my body and happy to be ME, exactly as I am in this moment. I AM home!

I now understand that the words I say after I AM really do matter as they either expand me or limit me. I have experienced both. I now consciously choose the ones that expand me.

Today some of the words that I say after I AM – unstoppable, limitless, brave, worthy, strong, resilient, capable, willing, compassionate, kind, loving, curious. I don't just say these words, I believe them. As the words changed, my inner and outer lives became congruent, and I am creating my truly "perfect" life.

Now it is your turn. What words do you use after I AM? Do they support the reality you desire? Do they expand you or limit you? Choose your words carefully as they are powerful...

Jenn Eastwood

JENN EASTWOOD

During her long career as a Certified Public Accountant (CPA) and auditor, Jenn Eastwood found herself increasingly obsessed with understanding what inspired and motivated people to overcome and bounce back from both personal and professional challenges.

Jenn is no stranger to the challenges professional women face as they try to juggle their personal and professional lives "perfectly". She has also experienced significant pain from life altering events including infidelity, divorce, abusive relationships, chronic pain, and losing her husband to suicide. In each challenging situation that Jenn faced, she focused on the opportunities.

Jenn left her safe career to become a Certified Fearless Living Coach and follow her passion of helping her clients turn their pain and challenges into opportunities and not only bounce back but bounce forward into a stronger, wiser, and more authentic version of themselves.

To learn more about Jenn, visit www.authenticallyyou.com
You can also connect with her at:
https://www.linkedin.com/in/jenneastwoodcpa/
https://www.facebook.com/jenn.l.eastwood

Scan the Code with your smartphone
to view a message from Jenn Eastwood

CONVERSATIONS WITH THE DIVINE ON LIFE'S PURPOSE

· · · ✦ ✦ ✦ · ·

By Joia Jitahidi

"The Purpose of this life is to find your Self. Know your Self. Feel the throb of the Ocean of God's presence in your Heart... we connect the little joy of the soul with the vast joy of the Spirit..."

Paramahansa Yogananda
Spiritual Diary
2013 Printing

CHAPTER 9

CONVERSATIONS WITH THE DIVINE ON LIFE'S PURPOSE

· · ✦ ✦ ✦ ✦ · · ·

By Joia Jitahidi

When I ask a question, I fully expect an answer. I remember how that first happened.

As a young child of three, one night, my mother said, "Let's say our prayers together. Here, on our knees, like this – beside your bed. My mother taught me to pray like this and just talk to God."

We knelt together by my bed, and I listened to her praying, and I thought, YES! I see. And then it was my turn. I began to talk openly to God for the first time.

First, I thanked God for today – "Thank you for today. I really like it when the sun shines, and the grass is soft between my toes, and our dog Spot plays with me like he did today. Mother's roses are beautiful all around the arch. And the lemonade was perfect today. Thank you!" I always began by sharing God's everyday blessings – health, air, the beauty around me, flowers, music, books – and especially my beautiful dollies.

Then, I prayed for others – especially those I felt had hurt my feelings or harmed me in any way. My brothers were constantly in this part of my prayer.

With my mother's guidance, I knew I could ask questions, ask about some curiosity, or ask for help from God. For things rather than "Why?" questions. Mother never asked "Why?" questions. Yet, I could ask for help with how to do a better "cartwheel."

Lastly, I again thanked God for the personal things I knew He was doing just for me. As I chatted, I remembered even more fulfilled prayers, so I thanked God some more.

On my knees beside my mother that night, heads bowed, quietly talking, I began a dialogue with God that has continued TO THIS DAY. I have come to understand God as Source – the foundation of my life force that I depend on, where I always turn.

I thought everyone talked to God. All these years, I imagined that everyone was listening, hearing, and looking for "signs" as God's reply. I trust s/he is always listening to us and always responds. When I ask a question, I expect an answer from God. So, when my Partners and I chose to focus on Life Purpose for our webinars and seminars to broaden the appeal for Inspiration, I was Excited.

As usual, I immediately turned to Source with my question: "What is Life's Purpose?" The answer: Deafening Silence.

So, into my sacred space I go – pictures, crystals, candles, warmth – and while I sit facing the beauty of the altar, I ask, "What is one's Life Purpose?" More silence. I am beginning to get worried – a bit. I thought, *Come on, guys.*

Next, I called on my spirit guides. I gave it another day, another week! Nothing, silence.

So, I call on the BIG Guns!! – My entire line of Gurus – Self-Realized Ascended Masters, all whom I know personally. I rarely present worldly things, material, easy stuff to them; however, this disappointment, my estrangement from Source, impacts not only me but also our business and my partners. Until this moment, I always deliver because I always have Source.

I sit in front of their pictures – all six of them – look them in the eye and ask my question, "What is Life's Purpose?"

Silence.

Now I am SCARED!! I repeat, "What is the Purpose of Life?"

In a whole month of asking, I am learning little and knowing almost nothing about Life's Purpose.

Now I am wondering, who is punishing me? Have I done something wrong? Am I no longer in touch with Source? Has God stopped talking with me? Why? I am questioning everything. I wonder how people live without feeling close to Source. I am losing all confidence. I am beginning to feel alone, abandoned, confused.

How can this be? What is going on? Am I in trouble?

Our class is only two weeks away, and I have promised to teach what Life's Purpose is all about. I believed I could ensure that everyone can know and live their life's purpose. And now I am in uncharted waters, unable to identify even MY Life Purpose!

So, I sit and begin to write for hours – rubbish, platitudes, all echoes of others' thoughts – nothing new. Then, finally, I surrender to the truth. "I do not know!" I am now many weeks into the Silence.

I look up "purpose" in the Webster-Merriam Dictionary and read aloud: "The central motivating aims of your life – the reasons you get up in the morning. Purpose can guide life decisions, influence behavior, shape goals, offer a sense of direction and create meaning. For some people, purpose is connected to vocation – meaningful, satisfying work."

That definition of purpose sounded familiar, like things I have heard before, and still, I continued to peer into the new unknown.

I did NOT KNOW the Purpose of Life. Is it to entertain God? Maybe? How would I know for sure?

I found myself crying, sobbing, feeling adrift, and so miserably isolated in this place of separation, of aloneness that I had never felt before. How do people live with this despair?

I gave up! Surrendered – throwing myself on the bed, I cried one more time: "What is the Purpose of Life?" In the yawning silence, I felt destitute, sliding on the surface in the many ways of the world. I had heard of this sense of no truth! I owe all my friends and clients a profound apology. I had no idea. This loneliness. This absolute FEAR. ANGER. And HURT that goes deep within. NOT knowing what to do – not hearing the solace of God's Whisper. I am so alone.

At last, in pure desperation, with all the sincerity of a child – finally – I called to the Muses, the personification of Inspiration. I called on Inspiration Herself to come to me. AHHHHHH

MY SPECIAL GOD-GIVEN Process – OUR PROCESS!! – to share with the world.

I asked Inspiration Herself. I called on Inspiration to help me, please. I said:

> "Muses of Mine, Come to me
> And Open My Heart,
> that I might SEE, FEEL, and FLOURISH.
> Muses Come."

And I distinctly heard:

> "You are uniquely imbued with a quality of the
> Divine BY the Divine.
> You are here to express, experience, share, and explore this Quality.
> You have been chosen to come on earth at THIS time to share your
> Gift, your Divine Quality.
> This is your Life's Purpose. Share your Gift."

> Each Life is Unique! Each Life is a new expression,
> an extraordinary journey.
> Each Expression is Sublime!

Sublime defined:

> "To Elevate to a high degree of moral or spiritual purity or excellence. Of such excellence, grandeur, or beauty as to inspire great admiration or awe."

THIS Sublime Expression IS our Life's Purpose.

At last, I could hear the truth. Finally, I could hear the whisper of my Higher Self! Then, I recognized God's Whisper. Home, again.

Now, I share Life's Purpose and the Muses – INSPIRATION with ALL.

I am excited and honored to share with you all of what I am learning – the Muses are the personification of Inspiration. And I have been asked by Source to spread these NEW Muses all over the planet.

And that's another Story. To Be Continued...

Joia Jitahidi

JOIA JITAHIDI

Joia Jitahidi is an Inspiration to all she meets. So naturally, her gift is Inspiration – a rarely used, newly available Energy field for the world.

She has "downloaded" New Muses, which are the personification of Inspiration. Together with her business partner, she eloquently explains everything in her latest book, *Inspiration the Answer*, where she introduces Inspiration – the Muses as a daily companion.

Her story introduces you to the Divine Purpose Path for an easy and fun way to manifest, with a map for your journey to connecting with your life's purpose. Other books by Joia include *Making Austin Work: A Book of INSIDE Information about the World of Work in Austin, Texas*. Joia later wrote for the World of Work, *Intuitive Management: Creating an Inspired Workforce, 2004*.

Working with numerous executives and managers from not-for-profit, multi-billion-dollar, private, and public companies, Joia specializes in creating thriving teams, collaborative work environments, and progressive leadership development.

Contact: joia@inspirationtheanswer.com
Website: https://www.inspirationtheanswer.com/
LinkedIn: https://www.linkedin.com/in/joia-jitahidi-5399a33/

Scan the Code with your smartphone
to view a message from Joia Jitahidi

BLESSINGS

By Jyothsna Muppalla

"If an inspiring thought occurs to me in the ordinary way, I know it comes from the mind; but if it appears suddenly, like a flash of light, I know it comes straight from God through intuition."

~ Sri Gyanamata
God Alone

CHAPTER 10

BLESSINGS

· · · ✦ ✦ ◆ ✦ ✦ · · ·

By Jyothsna Muppalla

It was a very proud day for our family, as the Animal Welfare Department in the state was honoring my father for his Humanitarian work. He had contributed immensely as a businessman and a veterinarian.

My dad decided that my uncle and I would accompany him to the award ceremony, a five-hour trip from home for us and the driver. My daughter was supposed to accompany us, but I felt she shouldn't skip school, so we had to leave her. Since there would be many visiting doctors at the award ceremony, my dad made sure he packed the car with medicine samples for gifts. Bulky boxes surrounded me in the back seat.

We started early at 3:30 am. I was looking forward to the ride as we would cross beautiful hills with wildflowers. We started chatting as we got on the highway, then we all began dozing off, except for our driver. For some reason, I woke up at dawn, just before the sun was coming over the horizon. I looked out the window and realized we were going pretty fast. From the corner of my eye, I saw something approaching that froze me. I remember yelling the driver's name, but I am pretty sure he did not hear me as he was asleep at the wheel. I did not even get out the full warning when I saw that we were heading fast into a big tree.

Before I lost consciousness, the last thing I remember was the pressure of the boxes all over me and my head hitting the front dashboard while the car was spinning around and around.

It just so happened that when the car landed upside down in the ditch adjacent to the road, the day workers nearby saw what happened and rushed to help us. They found my dad, uncle, and the driver and quickly pulled them out of the upside-down car. However, none of the workers knew that I was still in the car.

Even when I regained consciousness, I could not move. I remember hearing a faint voice shouting, "There is one more person in the car!" They opened the back trunk of the squished car, cleared the boxes, and pulled me out. I was numb in both body and mind.

As they helped me out of the car, I looked down, and through my swollen eyes, I saw lots of blood smearing my favorite white dress. I could taste blood in my mouth, and bruises marked my hands and feet. To this day, I do not know why there was so much blood.

Tears rolled down my cheeks as this was a scary experience. Fear overwhelmed me because I didn't know if everyone else was okay, so I was glad the workers assured me they were safe.

Looking around, I saw many people, but what caught my attention was the crying driver with a nosebleed, my uncle, conscious, lying flat on the ground, and my father sitting under a tree in shock. He had bruises, cuts, blood on his torn shirt, and he appeared to have broken his leg.

As my heart raced with fear, anguish, and disbelief about what I was seeing, I slowly walked toward my dad, who had tears in his eyes. "Are you okay, dear?" he asked. I nodded, yes. He said, "Thank God you are okay! What a disaster! This accident is so unfortunate."

I looked around more and seeing our wrecked car in the middle of a rocky pit beside the road, I realized the great distance our out-of-control car had thrown us down the highway. Then I noticed that beside the road was a steep hilly area, interspersed with sharp rocks and boulders, and by grace, we had landed by the road. I did not know what to feel or what to think. I kept crying with pain, thinking, *This is bad, this is bad.* Then, at that moment, a thought flashed through like lightning in my head, asking me, *Is it really that bad?*

Despite this mess, we came out alive. I felt a big smile beam across my face – I had never felt more alive in my life. As I felt my breath moving in and out of my body, I could feel that I had a second chance. My head was as clear as the sky. I could see the height from which we fell, the crushed car, the broken bones, and the bruised faces. The only thing I could hear was the clear voice of God – a voice of clarity. When I questioned, "Was it a tragedy?" I could not feel any sadness, even as I asked this question over and over again. My heart smiled inside. Gratitude and joy lovingly embraced me. The surge of joy was so strong, it was bubbling up from inside, and I could not conceal it if I tried. I just continued smiling and giggling with joy.

In this moment of receptivity, Spirit whispered loud and clear. I quietly looked around the sad scene and listened to the voice in my head. Things appeared entirely different to me after I repeated the question to myself, "Is it really bad?" Suddenly, I jumped with joy and turned to my dad and said, "Dad, Dad, we are so lucky and fortunate." My dad said, "You are right, you are so right." So, then we both had smiles on our faces. At that moment and through the following days, no one other than me and my dad saw the things we saw.

By this time, my cousins and brothers had arrived and were surprised to see that I was a happy camper, waving at them amid the turmoil.

I realized so many things around me that day – death's door, the vulnerability of our human life, the blessings in disguise, and the helping hands of strangers. I felt elated by the gift of a chance to continue to breathe, feel life, have joy, and live. I had never realized that simply being able to breathe was an act of joy. Joy filled my heart, and I could not feel pain. Instead, I felt gratitude. I saw a love invisible to the human eye and visible to the open heart.

I spent the following six months in healing and gratitude. I remember the invisible protection I felt and the pure ecstatic joy that was so evident that people wondered, "Why the big smile?" While they could not understand how I could be happy after a car crash, I could only see the joy of surviving the accident. I remember giggling and laughing because I was grateful to be alive and how good it felt to be able to breathe. Physically I always took in air, and now my breath felt fresh. It felt like every blessed breath gave me a chance to look at the gifts and the new chances, receiving directly and indirectly.

That fresh breath was inspiration for me to live my purpose and only my purpose. I knew I would eventually figure it out more, so it was okay not to figure it all out at once.

This life is more than what it seems to be. This precious life is a loving gift from Mother Divine to me. I no longer rush. Now I choose to enjoy what matters most in my life. I cherish the small things that give me joy and become even more grateful for every single thing.

I remember the orthopedic doctor telling my dad, "You have the best fracture," in the sense that if he had to go through something horrible and break a leg, it broke in a place where it could heal easily. Anywhere else, it would have been more challenging. Mother Divine takes care of things in surprising ways.

When I step back from the happenings of the world, I can see the grace and beauty of the invisible protection of Mother Divine. She holds me in loving care. In the silent cave of my heart, I remember to listen to her voice, embrace her, trust her love and know that all will turn out well.

Jyothsna Muppalla

JYOTHSNA MUPPALLA

Jyothsna Muppalla was raised in a large, traditional Indian family with an Eastern mentality and became a pharmacist. Drawn to explore the world and her spirituality, she discovered answers in the spiritual realm and increased spiritual magic in her life.

Jyothsna is passionate about building spaces for men and women to connect, share, and celebrate. She demonstrates how inspiration—the divine feminine aspect—returns magic and ease to complicated lifestyles. Jyothsna believes that inspiration is accessible in simple, powerful ways at work and home to identify life's purpose and do our best work. She recognizes the valuable nourishment of her combined Eastern and Western heritage through the wisdom of "we need a Western woman with an Eastern heart." Blending the Eastern empathic heart with the Western way of manifesting, Jyothsna supports teams combining insights in action in the world, allowing us all to flourish. She asks that we hold hands and uplift each other to enter the new golden age. She attracted the modern Muses in her spiritual quest and believes they are the spiritual agents to anchor inspiration. She advocates for connecting with the Muses and taking Divine Mother's hand to find our life purpose.

Contact: jyothsna@inspirationtheanswer.com
Website: https://www.inspirationtheanswer.com/
https://www.linkedin.com/in/jyothsna-muppalla-85111316/

Scan the Code with your smartphone
to view a message from Jyothsna Muppalla

Forever Changed

By Kirkland Jones

"Smooth seas do not make skillful sailors."

~ African Proverb

CHAPTER 11

FOREVER CHANGED

· · ✦ ✦ ✦ ✦ · ·

By Kirkland Jones

The news flash that the company was days away from closing its doors hit us like a bombshell!

Stunned by our company president's announcement, you could have heard a pin drop as we mentally processed the impact of 400 jobs lost, and the futures of many families suddenly in jeopardy. As the head of household for my family of four, I wondered how I would break this news to them.

Now part of a Fortune 1000 company, my manufacturing employer had grown from humble beginnings 60 years earlier in a garage on the northwest side of Chicago. The current environment was a multi-cultural mixture of home-grown, highly skilled, and semi-skilled machine shop specialists on one hand; a sophisticated customer-facing team that covered the globe on the other; and a team of support folks like me in the middle. Our belief that we offered the best products and best value in the marketplace was our common bond. Periodic visits from our inventor/founder, who was well in his 80s, helped us feel connected to this legacy, even as we sought to excel in the present and future.

We knew the corporate raiders from Wall Street who had swooped in to buy and "right-size" our corporate parent a year earlier didn't share our view about our business. But two companies from within our industry did, and one of them had just reached an agreement with these Wall Street financiers to acquire us and then merge our two companies. With that deal nearly wrapped up, how could it be that we were closing?

It was a convoluted story. Of our two suitors, the loser had convinced a judge to issue a temporary injunction that not only blocked the winner from acquiring and merging with us, it also prevented our two companies from further contact for two years. Perhaps even worse, the Wall Street raiders who now owned our corporate parent had finalized their exit strategy and were set to reap rich rewards. Specifically, they had reached an agreement to sell our pared-down corporate parent in 30 days and walk away with several hundred million dollars in after-tax profits. From their perspective, our impending demise was unfortunate, but not at all their concern.

Bottom line: the predicament we faced was our problem alone to solve. If not, in 30 days the corporate sale would close, the Wall Street wizards would collect their winnings, and we'd be history.

His words seemed an acknowledgment that the grim reaper had slipped into the room and presented our 30-day pink slips. At least, as the head of Human Resources and one experiencing the heaviness of our leader's pronouncement first-hand, that's precisely how the moment felt to me.

And so began my first genuine business turnaround experience; one that shaped my career (and my thinking) going forward and helped to crystallize my passion for building great teams – dream teams – if you will. This would turn out to be my leadership origin story; and the first time I saw the amazing, transformative power that a collaborative, trustworthy work environment can generate to deliver financial, organizational, and personal success for all key stakeholders: employees, owners, customers, and the community. (And, fortunately for me, it wouldn't be the last.)

Looking back, it wasn't just the news itself about the business closing that was unnerving for me; I'd been in tough situations before. There being no identifiable path forward added to an aura of hopelessness. "We've got to find a way to buy more time," was the best idea anyone could muster. Thankfully, as the meeting ended, there was a spark of hope when our leader declared he'd somehow find a way to get us more time.

More information did become available later the same day. It was both hopeful and devastating. As it turned out, there was an outside chance the corporate raiders would entertain an offer to buy the company from a group led by our top executives. That was the hopeful part. The devastating news was this: a non-negotiable prerequisite for such a deal – if it could be done at all – was that it be fully completed in fewer than 30 days, before the sale of our corporate parent finalized. This meant instead of getting more time to somehow pull a rabbit out of a hat, we had even less time than we originally thought.

Although completing the process in time felt nearly impossible, the executive-led buy-out plan was our only option to keep the doors open and save 400 jobs. And the clock was already running.

There was a proverbial elephant in the room, however, and it had to be addressed. To buy the business, we had to convince our bank and outside investors that we'd be profitable as a stand-alone enterprise. More than that, our financial profitability would have to start immediately. Here was the problem: Despite our #1 market share position, we weren't having a profitable year, and hadn't seen a profit in the preceding few years. Core changes had to be made – and fast!

Increasing prices, wringing savings from the sales and distribution network, and slimming down administration were ruled out. Dramatic restructuring had already been fully implemented a year earlier to siphon costs from those areas. No further chance of immediate and ongoing savings of any significance remained.

The only viable pathway to profitability was to dramatically reduce manufacturing costs. Traditionally, that approach was almost synonymous with headcount reductions and layoffs of union employees. But reducing union headcount wasn't a good answer because the financial projections we'd be presenting to investors required high levels of production volume; and that meant maintaining, or even enhancing, our skilled workforce.

The executives in the room turned to me, as the head of Human Resources. "Can we get the union to accept pay cuts in the contract to save the company?" they asked. "And get it done in time?"

Their questions were hopeful, yet skeptical. Unspoken was the universally accepted presumption that pay and benefits cuts for union employees were a required source of potential savings – and offered our only hope for success.

There were inherent risks. Neither the union leadership nor our union employees had an inkling a crisis was at hand. Would they recover from their initial shock and still trust management enough to agree to cuts in their own pay and benefits? Those in the room were hopeful, yet doubtful.

My perspective and underlying assumptions were different from everyone else's, and they led me to believe there was a better path forward. I was sure there were significant savings opportunities through improved teamwork that would deliver the manufacturing cost reductions needed, and eliminate the need to cut jobs, pay, or benefits.

Executives were unconvinced but willing to hear me out. Traditional mindsets may have previously blinded us, I argued, but the team effectiveness changes I envisioned could be quantified and then dollarized using our current quality and production metrics. Engaging others in this inquiry would likely identify more improvements. As important, a solution that didn't include cuts in jobs, pay, or benefits was one I could get the union leadership and its members to accept.

I can only speculate about why our president agreed to try my alternate approach, but he did. Following some quick and insightful work by our financial analysts, their numbers validated my perspective. They confirmed the savings from getting improved team process language into a new union contract would equal or exceed the savings from cutting jobs, pay or benefits.

This meant, for the very first time, executive leadership would bet on effective team collaboration as the secret sauce for achieving breakthrough financial results.

To me, the most difficult first step was now behind us. We had a framework for a new agreement that would represent a win for the key stakeholders. Investors and owners would see credibly reduced manufacturing costs and a new enterprise poised to make a profit; employees' jobs, pay, and benefits would be protected (union and non-union); and the union's leadership would also play an important role.

As a second step, we would ensure there was curated space for everyone to be kept in the loop and also participate in the ongoing dialogue, consistent with their formal and informal roles. At a minimum, we wanted everyone to feel they could ask questions and get straight answers right away.

Only 17 days were actually available to complete the contract negotiations process and gain ratification by union members. Memorably, our perception of this tight timeframe as a huge problem shifted to appreciating the value it added to the change process. As a third step, we leveraged the tight timeline to create a sense of urgency that helped keep all of us consistently engaged in honest, productive, time-saving dialogue.

Negotiations with the union were predictably intense, and achieving a successful contract wasn't easy. The union membership first rejected the company's final contract offer, over their own leadership's strong recommendation to accept it. It took an extended face-to-face, drama-laden, personal encounter between the entire rank and file, our company president, and me on the last possible day – the 17th day itself – to gain the winning ratification vote on the second try.

Shortly thereafter, once comfortable that union leaders and employees were fully supportive of the stand-alone enterprise, investor support was locked down and the executive-led buyout successfully closed.

Leveraging this "fight of our lives" experience, our new company became profitable on a month-to-month basis almost immediately. One year later, the company earned its first profit in years. And the record of profitability continued for years thereafter. What a turnaround!

Financial success and 400 jobs saved were only two parts of the full story. Our shared experience delivered other valuable and unexpected revelations and benefits:

- It forged deeper relationships between us. We knew we were capable of achieving greater things when we worked together.
- It clarified that our future success depended on whether we continued to work in fresh, collaborative ways. This included individuals, departments, organizational levels, plus union and non-union interactions.
- New leaders emerged from all over the company, employees began recommending top talent they knew to join us, and our customers became more pleased with the support and service we provided.
- Most astounding to me was how it all felt. The work itself felt easier, more energizing, and more rewarding. This, to me, was the most amazing discovery.

Finally, during the first few months of our financial turnaround, I found myself scratching my head and wondering, "What just happened here?" How is it that the _same_ people, working in the _same_ surroundings, and producing the <u>same</u> products are now delivering successful business results when we couldn't do it before no matter how hard we tried?

Some solid answers surfaced, but more questions followed: Why did it take such a harrowing experience to cause us to operate in this new way? Is it possible such dynamic outcomes can be generated "on-demand" when needed, rather than only in response to a life-or-death crisis? How can we keep our success going and distill our learning into a leadership and management playbook? In the years since, no matter the industry or organization, I've remained engaged in a serious inquiry regarding these and related questions.

Such a whirlwind experience! It re-shaped my thinking, refined the direction of my career in business and Human Resources, and fueled my natural curiosity about great teams. It also provided me irrefutable evidence of the transformative impact that trustworthy, collaborative work environments have on building sustainable business success. Now, perhaps even more than then, I feel fortunate to have participated in a success that only a high-performing team can deliver.

No matter the size, structure, or industry, the opportunity to help build an organization's high-performing culture is magnetic. Few experiences provide such satisfaction, personal renewal, and empowerment. For me, the practical and purposeful learning from this very dynamic, multi-dimensional labor of love continues to be a gift that keeps on giving.

Kirkland Jones

KIRKLAND JONES

Kirkland Jones supports business owners in building and renewing collaborative, energized work environments to achieve sustainable success and high performance.

As a life-long learner, listener, and place-finder, he is passionate about economic development, job creation, and business growth. Kirk is Principal Consultant for K.T. Jones Consulting, LLC, and creator of the online education program for business owners, the Team Success Roadmap: Six Steps to Building Your Dream Team.

He has performed in Human Resources leadership roles in a variety of business environments, including in turnaround, start-up, family-owned, Fortune 500, and private equity-owned organizations. His successful experience encompasses the manufacturing, banking, construction services, commercial printing, and healthcare industries. In addition to coaching and mentoring leaders, managers, and employees at all levels, Kirk has served as the chief human resources executive for three companies. He resides with his family in Chicago, Illinois.

Website: www.teamsuccessroadmap.com
Contact: ktjones@teamsuccessroadmap.com
Instagram: @teamsuccessroadmap
LinkedIn: www.linkedin.com/in/kirklandtjones

Scan the Code with your smartphone
to view a message from Kirkland Jones

MIGHTY MIDGET AND STARS

By Lee Atherton

*"It is only when there is chaos within
that you can give birth to a shining star."*

~ Frederick Nietzsche

CHAPTER 12

Mighty Midget and Stars

· · ✦ ✦ ✦ · ·

By Lee Atherton

Did you have one of those fun grown-ups when you were growing
up who let you break the rules? Who took you on fun excursions
and spoiled you? Who just had a carefree kid's attitude and brought
lots of laughter and fun to your days?

For me it was the guy next door during the summer I was 12 years
old. I had the perfect full-time summer job babysitting Jen, the girl
next door. I loved kids, and for me it was more like hanging around
and playing than any kind of work. We had a blast! Playing games,
going to the park and to the beach, digging forts, swinging on the
swings, and hanging out with Hank.

Hank was a neat guy! He'd give us M&M's, take us to the store
for ice cream, play games with us, make us delicious lunches – and
he made me feel important. Finally, I had a voice! It wasn't the usual
"Children are to be seen, not heard" that kept me out of conversations.
For sure, I was soaking in all that attention. For once someone was
caring about *me* as a real person!

One rainy day when Jen and I were watching TV at his house,
Hank asked me to come look at something. The next memory I have

is standing frozen in the hallway with my shorts around my ankles and his mouth on my vagina. This naïve little girl had no idea what the heck was going on! But I did sense that it was wrong. Very wrong! There were other times that summer… the day he told me how much he loved my body and took me upstairs to the playroom. Afterward he said, "There's going to be blood. Go down and clean yourself off." And the time he took my bathing suit off when we were swimming at the beach, then teased me and made me do things before he would give it back.

He must have told Jen's father, because he started too. He tied me up and did cruel things to my body. And when my body betrayed me by being "turned on," I was reassured that this was a good thing to do. "Isn't it fun?!"

Yet I knew it was wrong. I could NEVER tell anyone about this. I was bad. I was trash. I was a horrible person! I was a slut! I was terrified.

And I couldn't stay away. Only when I was much older did I understand that these men were taking advantage of a sad, lonely little girl who had no friends, who never fit in, who was forever teased in her small world, and whose family wasn't able to provide the emotional time and nourishment a growing girl needs to be a fully realized adult.

Sixteen years later, I was a stay-at-home mom with three young children. I suffered from debilitating chronic migraines. Despite going to specialists, trying various medications, and keeping detailed food and habit diaries, we had not found any cause for the headaches. I was referred to a psychiatrist who was known for teaching relaxation and meditation. Maybe that would help.

One day after I'd been seeing him for two months and still not finding any relief, he asked, "Were you ever sexually abused?" I started to say, "No! Are you serious?!" But the doors to those deeply buried memories were suddenly unlocked! And over the next two months, the stories just kept coming! I was overwhelmed! I was scared and helpless all over again! I sank into a deep depression with never ending anxiety and panic attacks.

And then exactly one week before Thanksgiving, I remembered that time that Bill tied me spread eagle to his king size bed, had his way, and then left me there. Bruised, dirty, in pain, and scared, while he went to "get more supplies". He had tortured me physically, and his abandonment tortured me emotionally.

That year, I was the host of the family Thanksgiving for the first time. It was a big deal, and I tried so hard to have everything just so, hoping that I'd make my mom proud. And in some absurd twist, with no one in the family aware of my deep dark secret, I served that delicious, perfect turkey dinner to – and sat across the table from – that evil man. You see, he had divorced Jen's mother since that summer and had become my brother-in-law.

That was the first night I told my then-husband anything about what I had been through. And you know what he did the next night?! He freaking went out drinking with the *#@Hole!! It was as if I had told him some benign story of having lunch with him! I wish my husband had gotten mad, upset – anything that showed he cared. I was abandoned again.

I later told my older sister what her husband did to me. She said, "I know about that. I read your diary then. You're the one who came on to him, so quit blaming him!" I was 12 years old. He was a 30-something-year-old ex-marine. I don't think *anyone* could have stopped him. Let alone a 12-year-old girl!!

When she finally divorced him, I was the one blamed for the destruction of their marriage, for leaving my niece without a dad at home.

Soon after New Year's, we heard that Jen, his now-grown daughter, had disclosed that her father had abused her too! No one could understand why people thought that "game" with whipped cream that he played with her when she was a teenager was wrong! Seriously?! A man's hand in the pants of a teenage girl wasn't wrong?!

It seemed that stories of child sexual abuse suddenly began showing up everywhere. Or maybe I was just hyper-aware. At lunch one day not long after Jen's disclosure to my family, my mother and I were watching the news while my children were eating lunch. There was another one – another revelation of this heinous abuse. Mom made some smart comment about people being ridiculous. For the first time in my life, I talked back to my mother. I vehemently said, "It's not ridiculous! It's real! Jen's story is real!" And then in a hushed and shame-filled voice, I continued, "I know because that's my story too. Bill abused me that summer I babysat Jen."

I don't know what I hoped she would say, or even imagined she would say, but the words she spoke to me were some of the most painful words I have ever had to hear. With that look on her face, and a tone of voice that spoke volumes, she said, "You're not telling me anything I don't know. I knew it when it was happening. It's not a big deal. You're making a mountain out of a molehill. You just have to lay back and enjoy it! Quit destroying this family over something so foolish."

That was the first time I seriously contemplated suicide.

That night I found myself curled up on the floor in a tight ball of panic, falling into a spiral of anguish with no way out. I knew those pills that were just out of reach would make it all go away. But there was something stronger than that inside me. Something that froze my body, that wouldn't let me stand up off the floor and grab that bottle of pills that was just out of reach.

Over the years since, there have been other times that the challenges of life threatened to consume me. Times that the fears, the attacks by people I thought cared, and traumatic abandonment felt so overwhelming that I really didn't think I'd make it through.

When I was 8 years old, I was given the nickname "Mighty Midget." Running after a soccer ball without a care in the world that I was the smallest kid on the field, I had no fear when I just kicked that ball away from someone whose chin I didn't even measure up to. And I ran with that ball down the field and scored my very first goal – the only goal I ever scored in my soccer career. But what the heck – I'd done it.

Today, almost 50 years later, I *have* become that fully realized adult. Despite being told I would never amount to anything more than a secretary; I became a non-baccalaureate seminary graduate with my Master of Divinity. I have been a parish minister – one of those very people I was told was too high on the ladder for me to ever consider speaking to! I have been a sought-after hospice chaplain and funeral officiant. I feel comfortable in the first responder world where I am a fire chaplain, teach about resilience, and serve as a certified Crisis Response K9 team with my dog, Shadow.

The girl who once could only be a secretary has founded CoachRev @*the* CrossRoads where she is a respected end-of-life, grief, and resilience coach and international speaker. I offer courses on exploring your wishes spiritually, emotionally, physically, and medically for end-of-life and navigating grief. I also offer other professionals serving those at life's end courses in how to be resilient so they can keep doing the powerful work they've been called to do.

Without knowing it, I had been wearing that Mighty Midget suit of resilience for years. I kept bouncing back from pain and disappointment, from abandonment and horror. And I was NOT going to let that neighbor, that brother-in-law, my mother, or anyone else destroy me! I will just keep strengthening those muscles of resilience! "I am woman! Hear me roar!"

Maya Angelo once said, "I can be changed by what happens to me. But I refuse to be reduced by it."

We experience lots of change in our lives. Sometimes it is change that we plan and create ourselves and eagerly anticipate because we know that there is something good to come. Something that brings us joy, or fulfillment, or helps us reach our goals in life. And sometimes, those changes are sudden and chaotic, making us feel like we're a figure in one of those snow globes that's just been turned upside down and vigorously shaken! It's hard to see what way is up, and we have no idea what the next step should be or even how to take it. This could be the death of someone you love dearly, a job loss, or losing your home. Many life events can trigger that chaos, not just in our surroundings, but in our health, spirituality, emotional well-being.

If you find yourself at such a crossroad in your life, download one of my free eBooks. *"Tossed Pebbles"* is a prompted journal for those who are grieving, and *"Don't Let the Well Run Dry"* is a collection of daily wisdom for those who serve others.

You can settle all that chaos. With resilience, courage, determination, and a strong support system (including self-care!) you too will roar! Remember, as Frederick Nietzsche once said, "It is only when there is chaos within that you can give birth to a shining star."

Lee Atherton

LEE ATHERTON

Lee Atherton is a certified end-of-life, grief support, and resilience coach with over 15 years of experience. She is honored to help people "live their dying" by discovering the beauty in the process and the gifts to be found. It is her calling and privilege to journey with people through the white waters of grief, navigating the chaos until they reach the tranquil pool of stillness.

"CoachRev", as many know her, is also a compassionate officiant whose goal is for those in attendance to feel as though they have just participated in a powerful and meaningful experience led by someone who knew the honoree well.

Recognizing the demands of anyone in the helping or caring professions, Lee offers coaching and programs in resiliency for chaplains, funeral directors, clergy, and first responders.

After receiving specialized training, Lee serves public safety officials as a local fire chaplain and a Critical Incident Stress Management team member. In this capacity, together with her trained dog, Shadow, Lee supports first responders who have experienced a traumatic event. Shadow provides moments of joy and helps Lee provide comfort during an otherwise stressful time.

https://linktr.ee/coachrevlee

Scan the Code with your smartphone
to view a message from Lee Atherton

INNER AND OUTER CONNECTIONS OF HUMANITY

By Malcolm Grissom

"If you want to go fast, go alone.
If you want to go far, go together."

~ African proverb

CHAPTER 13

INNER AND OUTER
CONNECTIONS OF HUMANITY

···✦✦✦···

By Malcolm Grissom

It's 1991. I'm 21 years old, and I'm on the track and field team at San Francisco State University. According to university rules, no student can run on the team for more than four years, so today is the final meet of my college career. I've never won a race in college, but today I'm confident that I will win – I have to – this is my do-or-die. I need to show everyone that, despite my disability, I am still a winner.

When I was nine, halfway through the fourth grade, I had a deadly virus that affected my brain and liver. As a result, I lost my ability to walk and talk. Initially, doctors thought the virus could paralyze me for the rest of my life. But I wasn't going to let that didn't happen. Instead, after months of speech and physical therapy, I was able to walk and talk again. More precisely, I was able to shuffle from one place to another and grunt like a ten-year-old version of Frankenstein's monster.

Unfortunately, my mother saw my progress as a sign to send me back to school as soon as possible. That fall, I returned, not to continue the fourth grade but to begin the fifth. The kids at school treated me as if I was contagious, except for a few of my former friends, who were nice enough to bully me. To add to my anguish, I felt most of the adults in my life abandoned me. This ordeal went on for a few years, so I learned to cut myself off from the world.

By high school, my popularity turned for the better and my physical abilities improved, but the emotional scars remained. I needed something positive to assure me that I was normal. That's when I started running. I began by practicing on my own. Eventually, there was an opening on the track team, so I joined – and I ran – and I won. My confidence soared with the awards and recognition I received. Running was my freedom – the only realm where I felt power and control.

I ran throughout high school in Hawaii and continued after I moved from my mom's house to live with my dad in San Francisco. I no longer felt Frankenstein's monster – I was a speed demon.

Here I am – 1991 – a speed demon who lost every race since high school. I'm in the starting blocks for the 200-meter sprint, anxious about my start. The start of the race determines the winner. In my freshman year, my reaction time was like watching a snail climb a mountain! Over the years, it has improved, but today, I need it to be the best.

The noise of the crowd fades as I focus on the starting official call out, "Runners on your mark, get set…" The sound of the starter's pistol echoes throughout my body as I spring off the blocks. I fly around the first turn. I can't see anyone else – I'm in the lead?! I round the next corner, still no one – I'm going to win! I focus my excitement on the 100 meters to the finish line. I am so close, and that's when I feel this tremendous pain in my right hamstring. I slow down, but my momentum carries me down the track – all the runners pass me by without a glance.

As I limp onto the middle of the field, I hear the announcer's voice present the race results. Deep disappointment deflates me. Four years of spending hours on the track then hours in the recovery room; four years of training on sand dunes to build endurance and muscle; four years of sweaty, dirty laundry, for what? To lose?! My head coach comes over to congratulate me, but I don't hear him. Instead, I'm focused on my failure.

Slowly, I head toward the locker room. The sound of my cleats crunching on the cement stairs echoes through the hallway, and at that moment, it's the loneliest sound in the world. After my shower, I sulk home, favoring my right leg.

For the next few days, I wander through my life as if it belonged to someone else. I attend my classes, but my presence is pointless. I don't retain any information. I'm a lifeless shell of who I was before the race. I've lost the passion and the will to go on. Up to this point, running track has been the only thing that kept me grounded in college. Now my career is over, and I failed miserably. The social mask I wear portrays the image of a happy and content Malcolm Grissom. My eyes smile and appear full of life, but I feel like the ten-year-old version of Frankenstein's monster.

Several days later, I skulk into the locker room to gather my belongings. I move about surreptitiously, hoping to avoid my teammates. To my surprise, a school newspaper reporter confronts me. He is writing a story about me because I am the first runner with a disability to complete four years on the track and field team. He asks about my illness and about being on the team. I respond with the stock answers people give when they want to appear grateful but have nothing creative to say, "It was quite an experience. Too bad it's over."

When it's published, I read the article in the paper. The reporter noted that I was a psychology and theater major with a dance minor and now a letterman's jacket, representing four years on a sports team. He wrote about my illness and about how doctors once thought I might be in a wheelchair for the rest of my life. Then he incorporated quotes from my coaches and teammates. My coaches said, "Malcolm is such a delight and brings so much humor and spirit to the team."

One teammate said, "Malcolm's definitely not the fastest, but he's always trying hard, like in Aesop's Fable, The Tortoise and the Hare." Kevin, the fastest guy on the team, said, "Watching Malcolm come to practice every day and constantly work hard was an inspiration for me. Seeing Malcolm's commitment forced me to work harder, to be better." I was elated when I read this. For me, this was like the hare saying the tortoise inspired him! Now, I saw the end of my career in a different light. Rather than focusing on losing the race, I realized I created a new ending to Aesop's Fable!

This article caused me to redefine winning. Winning should not be defined by a trophy. Sometimes winning is simply showing up and doing your best. I needed my track team to remind me that I was a winner and that the victory is in helping each other succeed and thrive.

Throughout the years, I've gravitated toward solo pursuits, and I've always achieved a certain level of success. However, when I concentrated on learning from and collaborating with others, I blossomed, as did everyone around me. Each one of us is tremendous, like a tree. Alone, I have thriving roots and thick, strong branches on which I can build a glorious treehouse for one. Together, we are a forest, and we can sustain communities.

Malcolm Grissom

MALCOLM GRISSOM

If you describe Malcolm Grissom with one word, that word would be humorist. He is all about play and laughter. If you describe Malcolm Grissom with two words, the first would be humorist, and the second would be passionate. Actually, the first would be passionate, the second would be inspirational, and the third would be:

Supercalifragilisticexpialidocious!

Malcolm Grissom is passionate about entertaining, inspiring, motivating, and empowering people with the power of story. As an experienced and award-winning solo performing Actor, Comedian, and Storyteller, Grissom uses laughter to create community.

Through his public speaking and performance coaching, he shares his passion for helping individuals, especially those overlooked or discounted, find their personal stories and use them to achieve success. Malcolm Grissom applies his vast experience working with California's Employment Development Department and his knowledge of workforce development to assist people with career development. He is also studying for his master's degree in Marriage and Family Therapy because strong communication and personal narratives begin with the family unit. So, describe Malcolm Grissom with the words passionate, resilient, playful, loving, helpful, intelligent, inspiring, empowering, joyful, and, of course, humorist.

https://linktr.ee/malcolmgrissom

Scan the Code with your smartphone
to view a message from Malcolm Grissom

Your Worst Year Can Be Your Best Year

By Maria Mantoudakis

"You can be anything you want to be, if only you believe with sufficient conviction and act in accordance with your faith; for whatever the mind can conceive and believe, the mind can achieve."

~ Napoleon Hill

CHAPTER 14

YOUR WORST YEAR CAN BE YOUR BEST YEAR

· · + ◆ + · ·

By Maria Mantoudakis

It was Sunday night 11:45 pm on January 13, 2008. I was wearing latex gloves that came up to my elbows, and I was scrubbing the pots and pans from the super-difficult day that had passed. My mom had Alzheimer's, and that Sunday morning we had had an incident.

After she'd had breakfast, I turned on "I Love Lucy" for her and told her I was going upstairs for a few minutes to take a shower. "I will be down in a few minutes; just watch the show."

As I was still in the shower, I heard a man's voice downstairs. "Hello, is anybody home?" I quickly put on a robe and a towel around my hair that still had bubbles from the shampoo on it. I ran downstairs.

"I am bringing your mom home," the police officer said. "She walked to David Street and walked into someone's home. They called us and we are bringing her back. You must do something about this; we don't want to see her in the street again," the police officer warned.

The devastation was overwhelming. What was I supposed to do? Putting her in a home was not an option. There were times that she would not recognize me or my son, and she would hit us and scratch us. It was difficult to handle, and we were family. I just knew that as a hostile patient in a home she would be either drugged up or not taken care of properly. There didn't seem to be anyone around who could understand.

Throughout my life I'd viewed my mother as strong and someone who always needed to be in control. I was an only child, and she was so proud of me. It was as though she was living her dream life through me. She saw me as educated, independent, someone who could rule the world. I represented to her all that she ever wanted to be. The whole time, though I appeared strong, I felt so broken. My ex-husband moving back to Greece before our divorce had left me lost many years ago. Having to raise my son as a single parent and without any support from my ex-husband had left me overwhelmed. Being the only breadwinner for me, my son, and my parents had left me clinging to my career, always fearful of losing my job. On top of all this, having a mom with Alzheimer's and a fragile relationship with my fiancé had left me feeling weak with no choices.

Coming to the realization that I could not even take a shower without my mom leaving the house put me in a state of desperation. "Why did you leave?" I asked my mom.

"I was watching TV and thought this was not my house, so I just wanted to go home. I walked on the street looking for my home. Then when I went around the corner, I thought that was our house, but when I walked in and saw strangers there, I realized I had done something bad." She could see the overwhelm on my face and the tears.

I tried to reason with her. "What if I put a sign on the door that says, 'Don't leave'... would that help?"

"Go ahead and do that," she said. "It might."

My mom would go in and out of Alzheimer's. It seemed that there were moments that she could look back at what had happened and try to explain it. I wanted to hold on to those moments and was so afraid if I lost those moments, I would permanently lose her. But this time it seemed as devastating to her as it was to me. I took a piece of poster paper and taped it to the door. It said *"Min Fevgis"* in Greek, meaning "Don't leave."

Well, it was six o'clock and I had to go. My son was staying home, and he was going to watch my mom. My fiancé was waiting for me at his house for dinner and a night out, and although I had shared with him on the phone what had happened, it seemed irrelevant.

Although I had been engaged to my fiancé for seven years, my mother was not a topic we discussed. My fiancé wanted a life of adventure and fun, and I thought that bringing up my problems and issues would only lead to a breakup, another thing that I thought I could not handle. Going to his home every day helped me escape my reality, and I got to pretend that everything was good and normal. We told each other that the reason we couldn't get married was because I was taking care of my mother, and there would be no way I could support two homes. In reality, my mother turned out to be a distraction from the reality of that relationship.

I went to his house, and we went to the movies, then back to his house until he went to bed. Then I drove the 45-minute drive to my house. I walked straight into the kitchen and started scrubbing pots and pans, while my mom was in the living room watching TV, and my son was on the porch playing his guitar and singing his original songs.

As I was scrubbing the pots and pans, I could feel my mother standing next to me. I nervously looked up as she lifted her arms towards me. In her hands were her eye drops and the medicine she took at night.

"What now?" I said angrily.

She continued to stand there, and I knew she wanted me to stop what I was doing to put drops in her eyes and give her medicine right at that moment. "Why now? Why can't you wait until I finish? You know I will give you the pills and your drops before I go to bed."

I took off the gloves angrily, gave her a glass of water and a pill, put the drops in her eyes, put the gloves back on, and continued scrubbing. As she walked away, I could hear her saying something. I became impatient again.

"How dare she say whatever she is saying?" I turned off the water and looked from the kitchen into the dining room trying to hear what she was saying about me. The guilt still overwhelms me, because it turned out she was saying something kind: "Work, work, work... all this girl does is work," she kept repeating with empathy.

And as I watched her walk away, suddenly she started falling straight back. It was as though her body had turned as stiff as a wooden board. She fell backwards, and I heard the back of her head hit the floor. As I approached her, it seemed that she was not breathing. I ran to the phone and called 911... everything beyond that point seemed like it was in slow motion. The police arrived immediately, and the ambulance a few minutes later. They repeatedly tried to bring her back, but this was the night, right after midnight on January 14, 2008, that my mother left us.

Through the viewing and the funeral my fiancé and his family stood by me and my son. But they say things happen in threes. Two weeks later my boss called me to tell me that her department was being eliminated, and we were all losing our jobs. After 28 years, I was losing my job. But that was not all... a week later, my fiancé decided he didn't want to be together anymore. As he had done all the other hundreds of times, he had broken up with me before, he gave me the long list of things I had done wrong. It was always something I did, something I said, something I was that he didn't like. I knew that with my mother gone we had no more excuses for not getting married. And I knew that although we had blamed everything on my situation with my mother, most likely both of us were done with the relationship and not ready to take the next step.

My most important blessing in my life, my son, was still with me, and I was so grateful for that. But my parents, my fiancé, my job, and part of myself, were now gone.

It was so difficult to see this as a new beginning at that time. It felt like I just had three consecutive nightmares, and I felt traumatized, paralyzed and not able to wake up. How was I going to live without my job? How was I going to handle the pain in my heart from losing the love of my life? How was I going to handle the grief of losing my mom? 2008 had been such a terrible year in my life. But overnight, everything turned around.

My friend Wendy started bringing me to her Mary Kay meetings. There I joined so many ladies who were joyful and grateful for their business after having gone through hardships much worse than what I had just gone through. Going to these meetings with Wendy shifted my mind from desperation to hopefulness, gratefulness, and joyfulness. As my mind shifted, my world, my experience shifted.

I found it therapeutic to continue going twice a month to the Alcatel building where I used to work for my Toastmasters' meetings. It felt like I still belonged, even though I didn't work there anymore. And all the members of the Club were so very embracing. And it wasn't just the Club members. Everywhere I turned, there was somebody reaching out, offering their help. It felt like I was surrounded by angels; some were my friends, and some I could feel but not see.

My friend Stacy asked me to send her my resume, and when I did, she re-designed it. Her version of my resume looked professional and perfect. All of my friends became determined to get me a job, speaking to their employers and sending my resume to everyone they knew.

On April 1, 2008, I started my new job at British Telecom. They had matched my salary from Alcatel, and, after receiving compensation from Alcatel, I found myself financially better off than I was before.

In May 2008, I entered the Toastmasters International speaking competition, and was humbled to become the runner-up best speaker in New York and New Jersey.

In June 2008, we celebrated my son graduating from Middlesex College. I had an amazing opportunity with work to travel to London to meet with colleagues in the UK, where I got assigned to support the network of a major global company headquartered out of Switzerland.

In September 2008, all the new hires at BT met at a ranch in Texas where we were officially welcomed into this amazing company.

In October 2008, I was asked to travel to Switzerland for one week to meet with the Customer. Since I was in Switzerland, I decided to travel to Greece and spent an extra week there to settle some things with property I inherited from my parents. While I was there, I had the joy of meeting with cousins and family members that I had not seen in over twenty years. I also got to see my ex-husband, his new wife, and their two children. They were so happy and so was I; I was in awe of how perfectly everything had turned out.

Also in October 2008, the Dale Carnegie organization reached out to tell me that my evaluations from teaching their course had placed me in the top ten percentile of instructors around the world. 2008 ended with a trip to the Dale Carnegie Convention in Vancouver, Canada. There the top instructors were honored, and once again, I was humbled to be recognized as one of their top instructors. 2008 had become the best year of my life!

In March of 1859, more than one hundred years before I was born, Charles Dickens wrote, "It was the best of times, it was the worst of times…" and this was the year 2008 for me. It was the worst of times because I lost my mom, because I lost my fiancé of seven years, because I lost my job of twenty-eight years. It was also the best of times, leading to so many wonderful, surreal experiences. I got a new job that has been fantastic to this day; my finances improved tremendously; my son graduated his beloved college; I was honored for my speaking abilities and my ability to connect with participants in self-development courses; I travelled to London, Switzerland, Greece, Canada, and Texas; I had closure to my marriage. And I felt the freedom and courage of embracing the break-up of a relationship with my fiancé that was not meant to be, opening the door to amazing things to come.

In 2020 we went through the devastation brought about by COVID-19, and as we are still combatting the Delta variant, and there are social issues and political issues and environmental issues... everywhere I turn I hear someone saying how devastating life is these days. But what if? What if we knew that everything that happens in our life is a gift? What if we understood how being alive is a gift regardless of what is going on around us and how we judge it?

The great Jack Canfield says it is not events that determine our experiences, but it is our reaction to the events in our life that determines it all. So, what if our reaction and mindset is to embrace life and expect good? What if we always expect blessings, what if we judge everything as good, what if we judge everything as happening exactly as it is supposed to happen? What if we are grateful for being alive? What if we notice all the people in our lives who seem to appear during our time of need just to help us? What if we notice our angels? What if we notice the miracles in our lives? What if we see everything that happens in our life as a miracle that is about to bring us to our next level of Greatness?

How would our mindsets and lives be different if all these "what if's" were true? And what if I told you... they are!!

By Maria Mantoudakis

MARIA MANTOUDAKIS

Maria Mantoudakis is a best-selling author, award winning inspirational speaker, and a personal development trainer of more than twenty years.

Maria spent fifteen years as a certified instructor of a top personal and professional development program, and in 2008 was honored as one of their top instructors globally. The same year, Maria was ranked by Toastmasters International as one of the top two speakers in New York and New Jersey. Maria is currently a Certified Trainer of the Jack Canfield *Success Principles* Program.

Maria is currently a Client Lead at British Telecom, while writing, speaking, and teaching her course *Life Transformation Mastery*. Her best-selling book *Tsunami to Greatness* was published in February 2021 and became a best-seller in six Amazon categories.

Her company, **ReCreate Success Now**, offers corporate seminars, speaking engagements, small group training and personal life coaching to empower her participants to experience life transformation to their next level of greatness.

Connect with Maria:
Website: https://recreatesuccessnow.com
Facebook Group: https://www.facebook.com/groups/recreatesuccessnow
LinkedIn: https://www.linkedin.com/in/maria-mantoudakis-6979a/
Email: maria@recreatesuccessnow.com
Email: recreatesuccessnow@gmail.com

Scan the Code with your smartphone
to view a message from Maria Mantoudakis

GOD IS LIKE THE GRAND CANYON

Dying and Birthing Myself to Heal My Soul and Master Self-Care

By Mireya Alicia Cortéz

"There is no way in this life that you will ever fully experience the entire grandeur of the Grand Canyon or God, but you sure can enjoy your spot and the view!"

~ Mireya Alicia Cortéz

CHAPTER 15

GOD IS LIKE THE GRAND CANYON

**Dying and Birthing Myself to
Heal My Soul and Master Self-Care**

· · + + ◆ + + · ·

By Mireya Alicia Cortéz

"I'm going to run a marathon," I announced to myself as a statement of gratitude or delusion for having had enough physical and mental wherewithal to hike down and up one mile in the Grand Canyon on my birthday, June 23, 2009. I was 38 and had given up on life only a few months earlier, in February. There was only one other time when I considered "not living anymore." Neither time did I design a plan to kill myself.

I first visited the Canyon sometime between the spring of 1995 and 1999 in my twenties. It was before the internet with no way of searching online or googling to learn how to prepare for my visit. I had no idea what to expect and how to prepare for my visit. I now know there is no way to describe the Grand Canyon except to experience it for yourself. To me, the entire time I was there felt like an out-of-body experience.

I had never seen or experienced anything like this! At the North Rim, it was "in-your-soul impactful." My brain short-circuited because I had no category for the Grand Canyon in my mind. I was overwhelmed, dumbfounded, and in awe, all at the same time. I am doing my best to describe this first experience. If you have yet to visit the Canyon, you might relate to what I am saying through a personal experience that connects you to those feelings. If you have been there, you know how useless language is to describe it.

On my second visit, on my 38th birthday, I had finally broken up with myself. I had broken up with my first husband and forgiven him. I married him deeply in love when I was 23, and we "just didn't work out." I had broken up with my dad for years already and had forgiven him. My father was sick with alcoholism and depression during my formative years and was violent toward my mother. He broke us all, himself, my mom, us four kids, and countless others. I had broken up with a married man who I dated when I was 18. He had turned me into the church for the relationship we had that I ended. My conservative pastor and the church ostracized me at 19 years old for my young adult brokenness. I forgave them for that treatment. I broke up and forgave my rebound guy friend, who I dated briefly a year or two earlier in 2008. I even broke up with God.

Why was I still miserable and in so much pain?! My thoughts echoed loudly – they numbed me. Then, as I stood now facing the abyss of the Canyon, I spontaneously relived a dreaded memory of standing in front of another abyss at 19 years old – my church community – in the process of being disfellowshipped.

My memory of the disfellowship was the longest, loneliest, most remorseful, sinful state of mind I could put myself in. The familiar now somber faces of a few church friends who came to witness my punishment watched me from the pews. I had never attended a disfellowship before, and now I experienced the pain of my shame in slow motion.

"Me arrepiento por mis pecados. Renuncié mi pacto con Dios y con ustedes mis hermanos en Cristo." (I repent for my sins. I renounced my pact with God and with you, my brothers in Christ.) I nailed it!!

I would give myself an Oscar for that performance, especially at 19! Thank goodness for the times of rehearsing on that stage acting in church plays before. Now that stage was for my act of remorse, and I did it without crying. I walked down the stairs without falling, with my head downcast to match my solemn stroll. I plopped down in a heavy state in my new pew of shame. The pastor had the dreaded role of preaching forgiveness right after my disfellowship and encouraged those assembled to love without judgment. The congregation played their part with words and hugs. I thanked them under my breath. Still no tears.

Even though I was among other young women who lived through similar experiences, usually due to extramarital relationships, not all of us stood on the stage; some left silently to have their babies. I had the usual painful menstruation cycles that are nature's way of aborting babies not meant to be born. I waited for my baby for nine months, and it didn't come.

Before I endured the church community shaming me, I wondered, as many do, is God real? I had no safe place to process what I just experienced and express all of my thoughts and feelings. I could not yell; I could not cry – I was resolute in fighting God.

I made myself go back to church, demanding God to show Himself. He had been with me since I was five. Where was He now? For the next two decades, with every prayer day and night, I demanded that God show Himself to me. I wanted to believe.

Now, standing at the Rim, a little mouse scurrying by my feet startled me and disrupted my deeply remorseful state. After reliving that memory and reviewing my life since then, I felt small, like that mouse. But, unlike the simple life of that mouse, I was silently wailing, "I want to die!" In deep pain and sorrow, I was begging life for relief from my pain.

By then, I had been married for nine years, divorced for six, and my latest relationship at 37 years old triggered me back to review more deeply what had happened to me in my life as a child and youth combined with what I had done as an adult. I no longer wanted to be in my abusive relationship with myself. I no longer wanted to tolerate my put-downs. I no longer would allow myself to eat the garbage of my thoughts. I no longer wanted to make bad painful choices that brought me misery.

At the Grand Canyon, I died. Immediately, painful thought labor birthed me. I finally felt relief, release, love, acceptance, and inner joy I had never felt before. The afterbirth revealed questions: What do I want—what do I want my life to be like now? Who do I want to be? I didn't know yet. I only knew that I was ready for a life that was nothing like the one I had lived so far. I wondered and dared to dream. Finally, I silenced my thoughts and removed myself physically from the pain so that I could breathe into the dark crevices of my heart, the fresh air of hope.

I longed for a life of peace where my thoughts didn't ruin my days, weeks, months, and years. I longed for compassion for myself: "Mireya, I love you and forgive you." I wished to hear those words from someone, especially from myself. "You are not a bad person. No wonder you made those choices you did. The way your parents raised you in that traumatic environment with no help, no follow-up support, no one to explain the outcomes of your situation is why your thoughts are the way they are. Those things were out of your control. It's no wonder, Mireya. I can see why your life unfolded as it did. But Mireya, you are worthy, and those things should never have happened to you or your siblings, mother, or father. You all deserved better. Everyone, including you, Mireya, did the best you could with the knowledge and awareness you each had at the time. But guess what, Mireya? You are capable of creating a different life for yourself." Hearing my compassion for myself was incredibly healing. Before this moment, I had only heard myself say hurtful things to and about myself. My new words were, "Mireya, I love you. I am here for you. And I will not let anyone, not even you, hurt you anymore."

As I lay down at the Rim's edge, my tears watered the dry ground. I released my decades of inner pressure that had built up. I experienced the deep healing of surrender and forgiveness of myself. This place beyond words, beyond the body, transformed me from the person I was before into who I was becoming. I was about to be designed – by me.

When I hiked down the Canyon, it exposed me to how out of shape I was! I couldn't climb back out! Alone with my thoughts again, wonder flooded my mind about God's realness and grandeur like never before. The new me wanted to pursue God and hear His heartbeat. I longed to learn to love others and love myself.

Slowly I walked back up and out of the Canyon, and that was when I declared, "I want to run a marathon." When I returned to Los Angeles, I joined a training team to teach me how to run the marathon without hurting myself. I heard about the street cleaner called "the sweeper," which strongly motivated me to do my training to complete any marathon! My goals were simple: Finish – time doesn't matter –definitely before the sweeper gets to me. No injury – walk away on my own two feet (don't hurt my legs). Self-care – do the exercises!

On June 25, 2009, Michael Jackson died at the age of 50. I heard the news while on the trolly, on the way back from my hike. Millions across the globe mourned Michael's death. Although not a huge fan, I cried a little for him too. No one mourned my recent death. No one paid tribute to the series of my other deaths of self I have experienced in life. I now realize that these deaths to self are a natural cycle of life to be expected. We grow, expand, and most importantly, are renewed. "I'm gonna make a change. For once in my life. It's gonna feel real good. Gonna make a difference. Gonna make it right…" Michael Jackson's "Man in the Mirror" song became my anthem that year.

I started my self-care journey that day at the Canyon, and it has served me so well for twenty years. I ran my first of five 26.2-mile marathons in March 2010, finishing with one other member of my running team when we left our group behind, coming in at 6:12:48. In the last four marathons, I coached myself and ran those without a team. In all of them, I achieved my goals of being a marathon-finisher, walking away on my own two feet – before the sweeper came through at six hours and thirty minutes – and without injuries!

One of my life philosophies is that God is like the Grand Canyon. He is so vast that there is no physical way in my life that I can experience and understand Him fully, just like I wouldn't be able to experience the entire Canyon in my life. I accept that you see a different point of view depending on where you are standing on the Rim. It's no wonder why so many people have such different perspectives of God. I made up my mind then and there that whenever the paths of our lives cross, I will honor people's life journeys and awareness.

I honor your experience of life. I am curious, though – do you love you? Are you there for you? I hope you no longer let anyone, not even yourself, hurt you anymore. Be your priority. Be relentless with your self-care and how you speak to and treat yourself. I am here to remind you to do so.

Mireya Alicia Cortéz

MIREYA ALICIA CORTÉZ

Mireya Alicia Cortéz is the creator of Prioritize ME Time, a step-by-step online program for professional women that guides them to make every day a great day!

With her Los Angeles County-based 21-year career in public health and managing chronic and autoimmune conditions, Mireya recognized that professional women are overdue to care for and prioritize themselves. Throughout her career, she witnessed her friends and volunteers – despite experiencing pain –living their purpose-filled lives through self-care.

She advocates for the practice of self-care to benefit all aspects of life: home, workplace, relationships, business, and community. Since she visited the Grand Canyon in her late thirties, Mireya has practiced self-care for over 20 years. Her proactive lifestyle enables her to create a meaningful, purpose-filled life. She makes time with her nine-year-old son – who currently sports green hair – to watch movies, hang out, and play. In addition, Mireya prioritizes personal development, learning about new communities, swimming in the ocean (when possible), with occasional karaoke and dancing in the mix. Of Mexican descent and raised in Los Angeles with a life-long career in community engagement, Mireya is based in Memphis, Tennessee.

mireya.alicia.cortez@gmail.com

Scan the Code with your smartphone
to view a message from Mireya Alicia Cortéz

Now You Are The Voice

By Monique McDonald

*"Now I am the voice. I will lead, not follow.
I will believe, not doubt.
I will create, not destroy. I am a force for good.
I am a leader…"*

~ Tony Robbins

CHAPTER 16

NOW YOU ARE THE VOICE

· · ◆ ◆ ◆ · ·

Monique McDonald

I've noticed the most elusive thing many of us spend our lives contemplating is our life purpose. Why are we here? Who are we? What is our unique message for the world, and why would anyone care? Even when we think we know, we easily throw ourselves off track. Only one disapproving look or a few rejections can bring us back to face those niggling doubts and universal questions.

The more we step out into the world and speak up for ourselves, the more these doubts come to say hello and test our entrepreneurial spirit. I think this is why, when you look into the biography of the most celebrated of us, you will inevitably find someone who believed in them more than they could ever believe in themselves. Someone who always said the right thing when failure was the only thing in sight. Someone whose voice brought comfort, strength, challenge, and hope to support that person to move forward into realizing their dreams.

The person who believed in me more than I could ever believe in myself was my mother. She was my best friend and confidant. She was the person who jacked me up and held me accountable. She was the person who spoke in loving tones when I was hard on myself. While she was not perfect, she was a truth seeker who was constantly working to improve herself. She was a parent who dared to show me her imperfections so I could see that we all have them. She taught me that what was important was to accept those imperfections and work toward loving ourselves despite them. She was an extraordinary person, and she was my everything.

When I was a little girl, I wanted to grow up and be just like Mommy. She was vibrant and full of life. She was a singer with a gorgeous voice, and everyone loved her. None of that mattered to me, though. All I cared about was that when she looked at me, it was as though no one else existed. My favorite time of day was bedtime because she worked long hours, and that was when I got to see her. She would read to me and sing me songs. Then, she would hold me, tell me how much she loved me, and leave the soft light on because I tended to have nightmares.

One evening, when I was about six years old, Mommy told me that she had a surprise and needed me to be a good girl. She was going to sing a concert and had no babysitter – I would be going with her. It was the first time I was allowed to attend one of her concerts, and I was super excited. The concert was at Columbia University's Chapel in New York City, a glorious church with a huge dome ceiling. Somehow, I managed to get up to the balcony in the dome, which made her voice sound immense and disembodied, sending vibrations through my entire tiny body. I didn't know what was happening to me. I felt shaken to my little core. Mommy had transformed; she seemed to no longer be my mother. She was now a magnificent creature of sound and light.

When it was over, I raced downstairs. I pushed through the crowd of people congratulating her, and I tried to get her attention. When I couldn't, I started to cry. Finally, she stopped everything. She reached down and took me into her arms. Looking at her face closely through my tears, I asked, "Are you my Mommy?" It was all I wanted to know. "Are you still my Mommy?" I will never forget what she said. She looked at me like I was the only person in the world and said, "Yes, sweetheart. I am your Mommy. I always will be, and I will always love you. No matter what."

When I grew up, I did become a singer, just like my Mommy. She was my voice teacher and biggest fan. She was there when I made my Carnegie Hall debut and when I sang at the Kennedy Center in Washington DC. She was the first call I made when I won the first competition, and they nominated me for the first Grammy. When my career took me to Europe, we skyped for voice lessons. Her voice was full of laughter when we celebrated my performances or full of loving encouragement when performances didn't go the way I planned. She taught me that when anyone waited backstage to get my autograph or to share what my performances meant to them, that I should give them my undivided attention and look at them as though they were the only person in the world.

Oh, she taught me so many things and was so much to me.

So that night in October, when they told me she was diagnosed with Pancreatic Cancer, I fell to my knees as though someone had punched me in the stomach. I couldn't breathe. It was as though the lights had gone out. I dropped everything and flew to her side.

The following months were full of what cancer brings: the hope that chemo will work, the moment her beautiful hair started falling out, the laughter when she tried on wigs, the nights of her screaming in pain and anguish when her body stopped being able to support her. My helpless anger at the situation boiled over in awful, embarrassing ways that would have scarred me and distanced us forever without our intimate conversations when I begged forgiveness, and she understood. Once, in the hospital, I became a murderous she-devil when the staff wouldn't give my mother the care she needed because she was obese and "dying anyway" – and finally, the moment of realization. The chemo didn't and wouldn't work. Then followed the surprising gift of hospice, where patients and nurses told me that conversations with my mother had changed their lives. Around the time her breathing and talks with me became more labored, I had a concert scheduled in Russia. When I told her I was going to cancel, she asked me not to. I was startled. She said, "Go fly, sweetheart! Sing for me and all of us who don't have a voice anymore." For a moment, she became the creature of sound and light I experienced all those years earlier from the dome at Columbia University Chapel. Then, holding my hand in hers, she added, "And remember, I am your Mommy. I will always be your Mommy, and I will always love you. No matter what." We embraced, and that was the last time I saw my mother alive.

I went to Russia. I wonder now if she needed me to go so she could make her transition. I got the call that my mother had passed away a few hours before the performance. I never told anyone. I sang for my mother and all those who didn't have a voice anymore.

I came home and did all the things you do when someone dies. Our family created a beautiful service for the hundreds of people who had loved my mother. We released her ashes on the beach. I did everything I was supposed to do. Then I collapsed into a darkness that nearly killed me.

They call it grief.

I had no desire in me for anything. I didn't want to sing. I had nothing to sing about. At first, my friends were quite sympathetic. Six months later, they kept asking, "What's wrong?" I said, "My mother died." They didn't get it. All I wanted was to be wherever my mother was. I could not wrap my head around living in a world without her. Anything that had happened before meant nothing to me now because I couldn't share it with her. Being an only child, I had no one; my father had died years before. Divorced with no children, I felt completely frozen in time, unable to move forward. I felt like a ghost. I couldn't experience myself anymore. Everything I knew myself to be no longer made sense. I realized I only knew myself through the reflection in my mother's eyes.

A year went by in this disassociated existence. I couldn't work. I could barely get out of bed. I got a roommate because I couldn't pay the rent. I was starting to wonder if my grief would ever end. Then, one day I was flipping through Netflix, which had become my best friend. I came across Tony Robbins' documentary "I'm Not Your Guru," and it planted seeds that jolted me awake as though from a deep sleep. Tony Robbins had a training center that taught his "Strategic Intervention" coaching techniques, which I joined. I saw Mr. Robbins using vocal exercises that, while they were good, I had better information. I had been a trained opera singer who sang over a 100-piece orchestra with no microphone, and I know how the voice works. What if I could help the next generation of leaders train their voices to remain strong so that they could heal and vibrate the world?

This sequence of thoughts and events set me on a path that I hadn't foreseen. While singing and singers came first, I now include leaders and speakers, helping them train their voices, present their work to the world, and change lives. It's my turn to be the person giving undivided attention and believing in others often more than they believe in themselves, just like my mother did for me.

When I speak or sing today, I take a moment to connect with all those who have gone before me. My darling mother, who guided and believed in me. All the ancestors who paved the way for me to be here. I am their Legacy – the voice for those who no longer have a voice and the tribute to their memory through empowering the next generation.

Hello again to those universal questions. Why are we here, and what is our purpose? Could giving voice to universal connection and reflecting our magnificence to each other indeed be life's purpose? What I know for sure is that when I am feeling lost and alone, the quickest way back to myself is to look around and see who needs help. When I give someone a hand, I let them see their best selves in my eyes. When you speak words of encouragement and praise to someone, you show that you believe in them. You never know who you will inspire and how that inspiration could vibrate the world. Take a deep breath. Connect to the love within you and speak your truth. Now you are the voice.

Monique McDonald

MONIQUE MCDONALD

Known to many as "The Magnetic Voice," Monique McDonald is a Grammy-nominated, award-winning vocal specialist and charisma coach. Initially terrified to audition or speak publicly, Monique studied intensely with excellent coaches to cultivate her confidence.

As a result, she celebrated with outstanding Opera and Master Class performances throughout Europe, Russia, Japan, and the US, including Carnegie Hall, NYC, and the Kennedy Center in Washington, DC. When Monique helps you uncover your natural charisma and your "Magnetic Voice," you benefit from secrets learned in over twenty years through High Stakes Performance combined with her unique coaching style. Her passion is inspiring charismatic communication and mastery of the human voice to empower entrepreneurs, speakers, and leaders.

Please Visit Monique's Website: TheMagneticVoice.com
LinkedIn: linkedin.com/in/moniquefmcdonald
Contact: monique@themagneticvoice.com

Scan the Code with your smartphone
to view a message from Monique McDonald

The True Meaning of Failure

By Nicki Chang-Powless

What if I fall?
Oh, but my darling
What if you fly!

~ Erin Hanson

CHAPTER 17

THE TRUE MEANING OF FAILURE

· · + + ◆ + · ·

By Nicki Chang-Powless

I was one of those kids who liked math and science in school. It made sense to me, it was logical, and it was easy. I barely had to study for it and would ace the tests. I would be the one helping others with their homework.

In fact, I had a side business in high school tutoring kids on these subjects. Back then, I got paid very well for my services. It was better than working at the local fast-food restaurant and coming home smelling like grease! I had a very satisfying job helping kids do their homework in the comfort of their own homes. And I was good at it. I was so good at it that, after I moved to a different city for university, my parents got calls from my students to see if I was available for help. Zoom would have come in handy back then.

When it came time to go to university, I naturally chose to go into engineering. My father was an engineer, I liked math and sciences, and a person can make decent money with a career in engineering. Sounds logical.

Everything was perfect until I hit 2nd year. Suddenly, the world of 'simple' got highly complicated. Math was still fine, but some of the topics in my engineering classes took me out of my element. My head started to spin, and I began to feel lost and alone. I couldn't grasp all the concepts anymore. I began to feel dumb. In fact, my high stress led me to drop out of some classes to lighten my load. Yet, I was not about to give up.

I enrolled in the Engineering Coop program where we could get work experience while going to university. I thought this was perfect – the university would help me find a position. I applied to what seemed like hundreds of jobs, and I felt like such a failure when no one would hire me. I couldn't even get an interview. Was it me? Was it because I was a woman? Was it because I was Chinese? I was devastated.

I eventually dropped out of the Coop program. My summer jobs consisted of receptionist and administrative assistant positions. In this area, I was a godsend for many companies. I had a unique skill – I knew how to use a word processor. Back then, we had 8" floppy disks, and the popular programs were WordStar, WordPerfect and Word. I made more money than the engineering positions I was applying for would have paid! Plus, I excelled at my job. In fact, the agency eventually sent me to high-level positions like Executive Assistants for Vice Presidents. This gave me incredible experience in customer service, boosted my confidence, and paid for much of my university tuition.

When I graduated with a Petroleum Engineering degree, I had tough decisions to make. Do I continue to pound the pavement and look for an engineering position? Or do I do something else? I felt like such a failure in the engineering world, even though I had a piece of paper to say I had a degree and an iron ring to go with it. In Canada, all engineering graduates receive an iron ring to wear on the pinky finger of their writing hand. When people see the ring, they automatically know you are an engineer. It's like a badge of honour linked to a brotherhood that gives instant credibility. Even though I had the ring, I didn't have the success that went with it.

One day I had the opportunity to interview with a large technology company. They loved to hire fresh university graduates so they could mold them into their perfect employees. I was their ideal candidate because they were looking for someone to help them break into the technical engineering market – someone who could speak the lingo and had the credibility. It was in the little ring I wore on the pinky finger of my writing hand.

The position I accepted was selling technical workstations and eventually corporate business servers to oil and gas companies. The company gave me excellent training and opportunities for advancement. That was the start of my corporate career.

Instead of engineering, I had shifted into business. I was embarrassed to tell my engineering colleagues that I was not working as an engineer despite getting paid very well. I also felt as if I had let my father down by not following in his footsteps.

I stayed in the corporate world for 23 years. During this time, I worked for multiple companies and was very fortunate to have experience in many departments, including sales, marketing, customer care, software development, and operations. I even made it into senior management! I had the tremendous opportunity to see the many aspects of running successful mid-sized to large companies.

After 23 years, it was time for a change. A tiny voice in my head said it was time to move on. So, I left, though I had nowhere to go. I had no job. I had no clue what I wanted to do.

Then one day, a colleague informed me that they had been laid off from their job. They wanted to take their severance package and start a business. They knew what business they wanted to start but had no idea how to start a business. Because I had business experience, they asked if I would help them. My exact words were, "Sure, why not? I have nothing better to do with my time!"

Two months later, someone else came to me to say they had been in business for two years and were not attracting the type of people they wanted to work with. Because I had sales and marketing experience, they asked if I would help them.

That's when I recognized that the 23 years of corporate experience, I had was not common knowledge among the small business community. My unique set of skills and experiences needed to be shared.

My business started by helping local entrepreneurs. Within three years, I was making such an impact on their lives that I began winning awards for my work and even became an Amazon bestselling author. Today my clients have expanded internationally to include the United States, Europe, and Australia.

My vision is to help small businesses around the world achieve their greatness and make their impact. Eventually, I want to start a non-profit organization to support startup businesses in underdeveloped countries. It could be through financing, education, or support.

When I look back at what I experienced during my university days and the feeling of complete inadequacy and failure, I see now that engineering was not the path that was meant for me. Each step I took was an uphill climb. Each door I opened would close. Each victory I had was small and insignificant. Now I see that it was a way for the universe to tell me that those failures were hints for me to keep moving and that there was something bigger and better ahead for me.

Sometimes things happen for a reason. We all need to step back and watch for the signs and listen to what they're saying. If it doesn't feel right, then it probably isn't. Trust me, you will know when it's right. It will be your destiny.

It's interesting how things turned out. My engineering training has not been a total waste. Today, I am doing exactly what I was trained to do as an engineer. I build things, and I fix things. The only difference is I work with companies and people instead of structures. Today, I wear my engineering ring proudly, knowing that I have made a difference in the lives of many people.

Nicki Chang-Powless

NICKI CHANG-POWLESS

Nicki Chang-Powless is a speaker, Business Strategist, and with her book *"Putting the Pieces Together: Your Survival Guide to the First Five Years in Business"* also an Amazon Bestselling Author. Her vision is to help entrepreneurs around the world achieve their greatness and make their impact by uncovering creative ways for them to save time and money, and ultimately, grow in abundance and make more profit!

Her programs have made such an impact on the small business community that she was the recipient of 2018 Best New Business Venture award at the SuPEARLative Awards and 2019 Entrepreneur of the Year at the Business from the Heart Awards.

Today, Nicki and her team of Business Strategists help business owners work less and make more by making the business journey simple!

Connect with Nicki
Web: NCPConsulting.net
Facebook: Facebook.com/nicki.changpowless
LinkedIn: linkedin.com/in/nickicp/

Scan the Code with your smartphone
to view a message from Nicki
Chang-Powless

CANCER WAS MY CURE

By Paul R. Palmer

CHAPTER 18

CANCER WAS MY CURE

· · ✦ ✦ ✦ · ·

Paul R. Palmer

The consultant asked us why we didn't come earlier.

"We've been trying to get through the National Health Service process for a year."

"Well, you're lucky you got here because your partner only had another six months to live without treatment."

· · ✦ ✦ ✦ ✦ ✦ · ·

I had always been a loner, or at least until I met my wife. In school, I avoided the bullies by spending time alone during breaks, keeping my head down and studying. I have always been happy in my own world. In school, I had the nickname TTME, the thinking man's ecologist, I suspect because nobody knew what I was thinking. When I completed my Master's degree, my manager said, "Now you've proven you're a clever bugger," and laughed. I remember another manager asking me, "You know it all. Why don't you use it?"

That made me think a lot.

My first marriage failed because of my lack of communication skills. We never really had a conversation ever! We agreed what to do, I did it, she complained. Of course, life didn't make it easy. Five separate redundancies aren't exactly the career you expect.

When I'm in a room watching the television, even if the room is full of people talking and enjoying social activities, I can watch from across the room and remain focused. The activities going on around me do not distract me in the least.

Everything changed when I met Ausra.

I still do not really know why I wanted to get to know her. These days I say it was stalking, going to lunch when I saw her arrive for weeks. I asked her out at the works Christmas dinner, and we've been together ever since, in sickness and in health.

Getting to know each other was interesting. When we met, Ausra routinely spoke Lithuanian. We communicated via Google Translate, a slow process as you might imagine, but it did mean we communicated and didn't just assume we knew what the other was thinking.

We had been seeing each other a few months, when Ausra said she couldn't cope with the travel any longer, that I was having to drive too much to go and see her. At the same time, her left side was becoming so painful that she couldn't sleep at night. There she was, working fourteen-hour days, and barely resting.

When we visited the doctor, we explained the situation, and she was referred for an assessment at the local hospital. They agreed there was a problem but that she had to be referred to another hospital with the capability of dealing with the issue. There was no mention of what that issue might be. I was quite disappointed with the system and the lack of communication.

In the meantime, I was continuing to work, travelling back and forth between the UK office and Denmark. I was in Denmark in November when I was told I was going to be made redundant, together with many others within the organisation. They apologised that my travel plans had not been cancelled since there was no one for me to talk to. I had a choice. I could turn around and go right back home to the UK or I could continue with the planned visit in Denmark.

I decided to stay but soon change my mind. I was stressed and worried, thinking about home and what was in store for Ausra. One of the people I'd been working closely with in Denmark offered for me to stay over at her house instead of alone in a hotel. I accepted her invitation, which helped take my mind off the situation and the uncertainty of what was I going to do.

I returned home with three months of gardening leave with full pay. (Gardening leave is when an employee is terminated and told to stay away from work for a certain period of time but remain on the payroll.) This was my opportunity to chase the NHS. We had already been waiting a long time for them to make any progress. Each time I called, I felt like I was being given an answer to go away. There was no offer to do something, no being helpful, no support whatsoever. I was alone again, just like I always had been my whole life.

I realised they weren't going to resolve Ausra's medical problem, that it was going to be up to me to do everything I could to ensure everyone knew what the problem was and to make sure someone actually dealt with the issue. I used my knowledge gained in the pharmaceutical industry to figure out who to talk to in the medical profession, how to communicate with them, and what was going to be needed.

Suddenly, I was communicating at a level with more interest than I had ever had before, spending time interpreting the words and ferreting out the underlying meaning. When one hospital administrator told me the notes had been sent elsewhere, I asked for all the details and the number to call. When I called, I discovered that the notes had been passed back to the previous administrator I had just been talking to. It was so frustrating, feeling like just a number in the system that had been placed on a waiting list. I'd heard about it from others, how you can go from the top of the list to the bottom, just by saying no once to an appointment.

I learned to play the game. This former self-appointed loner built a relationship with the different people I spoke to. I started to influence their behaviour to the point that one of them even called me back once to tell me that the notes had been passed to a new place – Guy's and St Thomas's in London. She explained that the reason no one locally had been able to take on Ausra's treatment was because of the complex nature of her condition. In this day of medical specialization, it's rare that one department within a hospital system is able to deal with cardiology, pulmonary, and orthopaedics as well as oncology.

I was shocked. Oncology. The word we all know and wish to avoid was out there in the open. Ausra had cancer. Should I tell her? Maybe she already realised, maybe not. I decided to keep it to myself, I did not want her to feel the stress that I was already feeling. I knew it could make things worse.

We travelled together to Guy's and St. Thomas's. I was driving of course; I knew we couldn't go all the way in the car so I chose the easiest station en route. Three hours later we arrived, a painful trip for Ausra but a positive one. In the waiting room, we both knew we were in the oncology department. I hadn't spoken to anybody. No one knew what was really going on. I was scared. What was the outcome going to be?

They started with the scans. Fortunately, the results came through in real time. We didn't have to return for another visit. With the constant pain I didn't really want her to endure another 6 hours round trip, she didn't complain but I could see her face. The consultant sat there, reviewing the data, looking at the scans, the x-ray, and the previous MRI scan. He explained to us what the situation was, that the cancer was growing and growing quickly, except he didn't call it cancer. He gave it a technical name that only I understood. Using Google Translate, I had to explain and describe the problem to Ausra. The consultant showed me the x-ray, explained how the growth was pressing on her lungs and potentially her heart although it wasn't clear.

That's when he asked why we hadn't come earlier and I replied, "We've been trying to get through the NHS process for a year."

He wanted another scan – a new MRI with higher resolution so he could be sure of the prognosis. I expected we would have to go away and come back another day. I was surprised when he said that he would arrange it there and then. That must mean it was serious.

We returned to the waiting room. Talking without showing how stressed I was feeling was an effort. I tried to protect her, but it didn't work. She understood exactly what was going on with or without Google Translate.

After the MRI, we returned to the consultant's office. He wanted to schedule an operation, and of course we agreed. I knew that smoking was unacceptable, so I had already warned Ausra that she would need to stop smoking and, if the consultant asked, she could tell him she had already stopped. During my numerous conversations where I had researched and investigated everything, I had also found out before we even got there that she would need have somewhere to go after the operation with someone to look after her or they wouldn't perform the surgery. I arranged for her to move in with me so I could look after her afterwards.

They offered a date in December just before Christmas for her operation, but she didn't want her daughter to always be reminded of her mother's death at Christmas, so she declined the appointment. On 21st January 2011, the operation was a success, the lump was removed, and she started physical therapy in the hospital.

When they discharged her, they sent her home with a bag of medicine. The morphine pump was only available during her stay while she was recovering in the hospital. She liked it of course, and I knew the pump had a restricted dose, unlike the boxes of Oramorph she came home with. I looked after her at home, making sure she took the right tablets at the right time. I attended all the appointments everywhere – in the hospital for the check-ups, at the medical centre for the dressings. I explained to the nurse which dressings we should be using. After all, when I worked in pharmaceuticals in the past, I had been part of the team that developed cannula dressings (used for catheter sites to keep them dry) as well as those needed to absorb exudate (fluid that leaks out of blood vessels into nearby tissues). We got everything we needed, and the nurse ordered whatever she didn't have in stock.

Recovery took time, but we had time. She was alive.

I was anxious for 10 years – watching, looking for signs that the cancer has come back. I took notice. Is that a sign? Maybe.

Now after ten years she has been given the all clear, and the annual check-ups have ended, the risk is now the same as anyone else. I'm happy, ecstatic, overjoyed, pleased I was there.

The experience changed me personally. I started to care what other people thought, what they said, what they did. I was no longer alone, and I never wanted to be alone again, not the way I had been before.

The experience changed me professionally. I started my own business because flexibility was key. I still needed to be there when I was needed. Now I listen to clients, interested in what they have to say, interested in their needs and providing for those needs, whatever they may be. I communicate openly, clearly, and not just by telling. It's important for me to understand first and apply my knowledge so I can help them solve their problems. To help them meet the patient needs.

Ausra and I have been married now for six years. I'm no longer in my own world. I'm no longer happy to be alone. I really do feel cancer was the cure for my loneliness.

Paul R. Palmer

PAUL R. PALMER

When Paul Palmer was in school, he wanted his own business as an inventor, to create something different. He moved through the first phases of professional life in a very opportunistic way utilising my organisations to further his career. He left the pharma industry for a few months and hated it which cemented the industry and chosen path.

Looking for how he could get to where h wanted to be Paul took over as Head of Quality when the incumbent left without anyone offering, he made the job his own and moved forward with it.

Change happens to us all and he moved through several different companies before landing a role where he enjoyed auditing and advising people on what to do and naturally gravitated towards helping the teams communicate, align, and solve problems, becoming known as a 'Mr fix it'.

Paul was only doing a job because he thought it gave him security. After the fifth redundancy, he realised he wanted to do his own thing and couldn't rely on a company for a pay check, he started his own business. Paul enjoys running his own business so much he will never go back, Paul directs, leads, and advises people.

Paul wants to improve the way pharmaceutical companies are run; he cares about the patients. Paul believes companies should be there to care about the patients, ahead of profitability.

www.paulrpalmer.com

Expect the Unexpected and Step into Your Power

By *Petra Contrada*

*"Just like moons and suns,
with certainty of tides,
just like hopes springing high,
still, I'll rise."*

~ Maya Angelou

CHAPTER 19

EXPECT THE UNEXPECTED AND STEP INTO YOUR POWER

· · ◆ ◆ ◆ · ·

By Petra Contrada

U niversal to all of us as we journey through life are encounters with unforeseen setbacks and challenges. Life is uncertain, and the challenges that come along with it can either make you or break you. However, no matter what you are confronted with, there is nothing that you cannot handle.

Things End Differently than Expected

It's a beautiful Friday afternoon in late March 1993. The early spring sun is streaming into my car and mere hours earlier I completely rocked a huge Train-the-Trainer meeting I ran on behalf of my employer – a large cosmetics company in Germany. I should be home enjoying a relaxing and joyful weekend. I should be celebrating. Instead, I am sitting paralyzed in my car. A cold sweat drenches my body and inside my head a whirlwind of anger and fear threatens to annihilate my normal sense of logic and reason.

Three hours earlier I had completed the first big event in my new position as International Training Director for the company that had hired me just four months prior. My task was to develop and launch the organization's first international training department. I had already done this very successfully in my previous position for a competitor, and I had established a reputation as one of the best in the field.

I had worked hard to do a phenomenal job and the week's event had ended with standing ovations from the participants--all of whom were national trainers for our subsidiaries in locations around the world.

Instead of being celebrated for my triumph, I found myself fired.

All Seemed Lost

When I had started my new job, my goal had been to make my mark and do my work to the absolute best of my abilities. Within a few weeks, I had been traveling around the globe and speaking to local trainers, marketing directors, and general managers. We worked day and night, to create new programs for the four different brands I had under my wings and although I had set myself a challenging goal, I wanted to prove myself with this new company.

My efforts culminated in this first event, which had started on the previous Sunday in the most prestigious hotel in town. I spent the week that followed educating, training, and entertaining those who had attended. I was proud of what I had accomplished. Given how busy I was, I had not paid much attention to the rumors that were rolling in from headquarters. I had been shocked early that week to hear that my boss had been fired. Little did I know how much more chaos was to ensue. The company was owned by a huge global firm and their management team had decided to move the International Marketing headquarters to New York. During the week which was supposed to cement my reputation, almost 300 people were laid-off. I began to wonder what would happen after my event: would they just let me finish it and then fire me or would they acknowledge what I had accomplished and transfer me to the United States?

Almost immediately after my event wrapped up, I received a call from the office to report right away to the company's new General Manager. *"Oh boy,"* I thought, *"maybe it's a good sign that I did not have to report to human resources like all the others who were fired. Maybe he'll offer me another job after all!"*

As it turned out, I was the last employee to be let go. I was already overwhelmed and burnt out from the intensity of the previous weeks and now I was left sitting in my car heartbroken and at a loss as well. I went back and forth between feeling hollow and wanting to scream my outrage. All my hard work had been for nothing. Instead of reaping the fruits of my efforts, I was out of a job.

I had given up my previous job – which I had loved – and there were not many positions available in Germany that offered international opportunities. In addition, I had just spent a great deal of money moving to a new city, and I was enamored with my beautiful new apartment. Everything had been going well for me and then all of a sudden, the carpet was ripped out from under me.

That Friday, I returned home in a state of deep shock. I didn't know what to do next or what the future would hold for me. I was angry and devastated – all seemed lost.

Never, Never, Never Give Up

As you would expect, I had a terrible weekend in which I indulged in waves of depression and self-pity. I oscillated between crying my eyes out and raging against the world. That was until I realized that wallowing in such emotions would not get me anywhere. I needed to pull myself together and move on despite my fears, worries, and outrage.

By Monday I had my confidence back and I was determined to leave with a bang. Instinctively I trusted that no matter what happened, things would turn out alright in the end if I made the right choices. Would my choices be guided by fear of failure or of the unknown? Would they be guided by a desire to stay in my comfort zone, or would they be steered by the decision to step out and expand into something incredible? What I had learned over and over again in my life was that no matter how difficult things may seem, one can never give up.

Stepping Out and Up

The next week I shipped copies of all the training programs, manuals, and tools I had developed to all of our subsidiaries. Saving the most important one for last, I prepared a final box to send to the company's US subsidiary. In order to give the package more credibility, I went to my former boss's secretary to request she send it over. She was not in her office when I arrived, so I decided to leave the package on her desk. As I was in the process of writing her a note requesting she send everything over to the Head of Marketing for the US market, I heard a voice with a distinctly American accent behind me say, *"Petra, how are you? I heard your event was a huge success, my two trainers loved it very much."*

I turned around and there he was: the director I was about to send the box to! Little did I know that he had just been appointed SVP of International Marketing. After some small talk, the fact that I had just been fired came up in conversation. He was sorry to hear of my situation and asked if he could do anything for me. The next moment, I heard myself boldly answering: *"Thank you, if you can help me find a new job, that would be wonderful."* I could not believe that I had the courage to ask him so directly! He gave me a thoughtful look and asked that I send him my résumé. Two hours later, I delivered a copy to his office and returned home with a sigh as I was not very hopeful that anything would come of our conversation. After all, people often make promises they don't intend to keep.

Over the next week, I repeatedly returned to headquarters in order to use the company offices and copy machine for my résumés and job applications. That is, until a secretary approached me and instructed me to stop immediately: the human resources department wanted me to come over ASAP. I thought I was in trouble for my continued presence in the office and use of the equipment, so I made my way to the human resources offices with a dull feeling in my stomach.

The Tides Turn

Once there, I was left to wait and stew in my anxiety, surrounded by depressed colleagues who had also been fired. Eventually, I was directed into the office of the new Director of Human Resources, whom I had never met. He looked at me in a serious manner and then said: *"I know it must have been a rough week for you, and I'm sorry for all the inconvenience but there is a new development... we are offering you the position of Vice President of International Training in New York. Would that be something of interest to you?"*

I could not believe my ears. Not only had he offered me a better job but he had also uttered the magic word...New York! My ears were ringing, my heart was pounding, and for a moment I thought I was going to faint. I had to take a deep breath to stop myself from letting out an exuberant, relieved shriek. I just barely managed to maintain my professionalism as I slyly answered, *"That is very nice of you, and I appreciate the offer, but that depends on the conditions."* Just one week later, I was on a plane and ready to start my new life in New York. As the plane began to land, I still vividly recall how my body thrummed with giddy excitement as I looked out over the city skyline. Spontaneously, the lines of Frank Sinatra's famous song played in my head: *"These little town blues are melting away...I want to wake up in a city that never sleeps... If I can make it there, I'll make it anywhere, it's up to you, New York, New York."*

Game Changers

Destiny is one thing, having a dream is another. When push comes to shove, I learned over and over again, it is you who determines your future. The previously described events were a fundamental game changer for me and were the beginning of a whole new and wonderful chapter in my life. I worked in the city for several years and met my beloved husband. We moved to Germany where we had our daughter and eventually back to New York as I was once more offered a new job there.

Unfortunately, upon returning to New York our life was again thrown into disarray. After the tragedy of September 11, significant loss and devastation forced me to shift gears and to transition not only to a new life but a new career. I dove into the world of Real Estate and was quickly at the top of the game – in the league of the top 5% in my area, leading my own team and my own successful business.

The climb to the top was a wakeup call. I realized that I was sacrificing my mental and physical health for more clients, more money, and more listings. This single-minded focus on external success in a field for which I held little passion led me to become profoundly ill. Just seven years ago, I thought I might not have long to live. But, to quote Dylan Thomas, I wasn't going to "go gentle into that good night." I knew I needed to do what I was passionate about, apply what I already knew and finally make the necessary changes to live a truly fulfilled life.

The results were so amazing that I sat down and defined my process to help other people to do the same. This inspired me to start a totally new business. Today, leaders, entrepreneurs, coaches, authors, and other experts hire me to step out of the ordinary into the extraordinary because most don't know how to lead with clarity, confidence, and courage and make the difference they are capable of making. So I help unleash their energetic powers to achieve the impact, success, and fulfillment they desire and assist them to reach their true potential.

The bottom line is: Never again settle for the ordinary when extraordinary is a step away.

Unleash Your Powers

What do you do when you face one of those tests of faith and courage that make life so challenging and at the same time so interesting? What do you do when you reach a crossroads, and you are forced to make choices that will determine the course of your life?

Are you playing it safe out of fear of the unknown? Are you staying in your comfort zone? Or are you following your heart and going where your dreams and passion lead you?

Most people need a wake-up call. They know what to do, but they don't do it. They want to jumpstart their lives but are stuck in the ordinary with no way to step into the extraordinary. Some have success but lack the clarity, confidence, and courage to make the big significant difference they are capable of making. Many suffer with hidden insecurities and doubts, don't receive the fruits of their efforts, and feel defeated, tired, and/or burned out. This ignites many internal limitations which keep people from stepping into their own power.

We all must step into our greatness to thrive and win.

So today, I am going to provide you with some proven simple yet highly effective tools that will help you to raise your charisma, create impact, achieve fulfillment, and enjoy lasting success.

First, start with exploring your status quo, motivation, and commitment to start fulfilling your destiny. These determine your priorities, and, deep down, they're the measuring stick to tell you if your life is turning out the way you want it to.

Next, it is vital to connect more deeply and confidently with your inner wisdom and step into a greater vision of yourself.

Self-awareness is the key. So, start by understanding YOU! The problem with a lack of self-awareness is that it keeps us stuck in our comfort zone. We know we long for more, but we settle for less, and suppress our feelings and desires.

Finally – and this is probably the most important part of living an impactful life – is to boost your magnetism. This is where we step fully into the extraordinary.

"Only those who can see the invisible can do the impossible," according to Albert Einstein, a man who clearly knew how to step out of the ordinary into the extraordinary. We recognize more and more that we are on the threshold of a new era and that old approaches are becoming less and less effective.

At last, I'd like to share with you the three keys to activating and lifting your Body, Mind and Spirit:

1. Gain clarity, confidence and courage
2. Develop deep understanding of the nature of your life's work and destiny
3. Take Action and plan your long-term impact

When these three keys are implemented in the proper way, the results are astounding.

Today I am grateful that I can help others to understand how to finally step out and step up. I invite you to step into your powers to "Be the Change to Thrive & Win" in life & business.

**We are in this together,
I am here for you,
you are not alone!**

Petra Contrada

PETRA CONTRADA

Petra Contrada is an internationally renowned speaker, impact strategist, success mentor to leaders and vibrational and intuitive energy specialist. She is also known as the founder of the Thrive and Win Success Academy.

Today, entrepreneurs, heart-led leaders and business owners work with Petra to step out of the ordinary into the extraordinary because most don't know how to lead with clarity, confidence and courage to make a difference. She is the guide for those who are ready to step into their power, to 'Be the Change, to Thrive & Win' in life & business.

Petra has become widely successful by helping other people to achieve greatness and abundance in their own lives. As the Leaders' Mentor, Petra's focus is on having a massive positive impact on 100 million people, serving her clients and community with the utmost excellence and integrity.

If you want to go from the ordinary to the extraordinary and you don't have a mentor who can take your hand and walk you every step of the way, go to:

https://www.thriveandwinsuccessacademy.com/mentorapply_30
to have a conversation with Petra to see if one of her mentorship programs can help you onto the next level in your life.
Email Petra @ petra@petracontrada.com
https://www.petracontrada.com/
https://www.facebook.com/bethechangewithpetracontrada
https://www.linkedin.com/in/petracontrada/
https://twitter.com/petracontrada
https://www.instagram.com/petracontrada.bethechange/

Scan the Code with your smartphone
to view a message from Petra Contrada

Unleash Your Genius

By *Yvonne Larson*

"Genius is the ability to receive from the Universe."

~ I Ching

CHAPTER 20

UNLEASH YOUR GENIUS

By Yvonne Larson

Y ou are a genius. Are you willing to unleash your genius? The most admired Entrepreneurs of our time, like Richard Branson and Guy Laliberté, always credit their genius to trusting their gut. The only way to do that is through absolute trust in your intuition. But it takes daily practice! You must pause, reflect, and introspect to connect with and engage this power. I've been engaging in and teaching this practice for decades. My obsession is that everyone realizes their value and their unique genius.

Your genius zone is magical. The genius zone is when one is in a state of flow or flow-state. Everything feels effortless. You feel lucky or like a magnet for unexpected, thrilling experiences. Many Entrepreneurs fantasize about it, but most are stuck in the hustle and grind of their business. They feel overwhelmed, stressed, and burned out.

So, what gives?! I intend to answer that with a few snapshots of my life.

In a conversation with Malcolm, I discovered the originating source of this wisdom and my obsession to share it. He kept asking, *why? But, why? But, why?*

First, I shared about the numerous losses I had experienced by the hand of suicide. Then, I shared, from the decades of evidence I had gathered from working privately with Entrepreneurs who were compromising having fulfillment in their lives for having success in their business. Finally, I shared my hypothesis that we use the wrong measures for defining success. Again, he asked *But, why?* Grateful but frustrated, I dug deeper. What was the real reason for this passion?

This time, with a lump in my throat, trying not to become emotional, I responded *because I felt unimportant and invisible as a small child. With all the volatility and confusion, I didn't know I was valuable or mattered.*

Instantly, I knew the source of my obsession to share this message. I saw a scene from my childhood with my mother.

We were stargazing in our backyard and having one of our chats that I cherished so much. Something was weighing heavily on my heart that I had to share. But how could I explain this deep desire?

I gathered up my courage to say, *Mom, I'm so happy that we're together. I love you so much. You're my best friend but,*

I paused. I felt hesitant to ask, *when do you think I can get a dad?*

Not having a dad left me thinking that something was missing, wrong, or incomplete. We had been through quite a nightmare with my birth father and his family. But, for the last couple of years, it had been just us. Life was so good, with one fun and exciting adventure after the next. Now, mom had male friends who were reliable, kind, and protective. One of them would make a great dad and husband! Right?

What she said next, changed everything!

God is your Father. He is everywhere, all the time. He is the best Father you could ever have because He's in charge of everything, owns everything, made everything. That makes Him the most powerful of all the fathers!

Yvonne, He knows everything about you. He's always with you, watching after you, caring for you, guiding you, keeping you safe, and providing for all of your needs.

That was game-changing intel for sure! Previously, I had a lot of evidence that the world was an unsafe place for me. Now, knowing that my dad was the most powerful of all the dads, WOW, I felt invincible!

Instantly, she upgraded my operating system and introduced me to my internal guidance system, my intuition! Up until then, I had been encoded, with the belief that life was scary, unpredictable, and unsafe. These codes were creating the perspectives, filters, values, and behaviors defining my life. Now, I could override those codes and stop feeling fearful, separate, and cautious.

Suddenly, I had a new belief of always being divinely guided. Now I felt free, powerful, and connected to everything. I would forever draw upon my intuition. This wisdom came through my mom!

Throughout my life, I've learned, the one guarantee about life is that there are no guarantees. So, when we grow up having all these codes installed into our system, it poses a vital question. What will you do when life feels like life is happening **to you** instead of **for you**?

The answer? Trust your intuition.

Your intuition is not a code. It is a gift from your Soul at your conception. Essentially you have your very own built-in GPS. This internal guidance system helps you course-correct when the various survival codes knock you off of your true north. You must embrace and embody your intuition!

For a moment, pause for clarification. Intuition has several different names like God, Spirit, Universe, Source, and the Creator. Feel free to call it whatever resonates best for you.

What dictates the frequency of experiencing the ease and grace of your genius zone is alignment with your intuition. That brings another memory to mind.

Years ago, my friend, Pam, said something that left me feeling a deep sense of gratitude, pride, and appreciation for my life. I was in the middle of a crisis.

Relief or resolution seemed impossible. But I kept listening to and trusting my intuition. I kept moving forward despite how bad things were looking. Then, all of a sudden, like magic, resolution came.

When I ran into her, she empathetically asked for an update about the crisis. When I shared the miracle, she remarked *Your life is not always easy, but wow, it sure is charmed.* She was 100% right.

Life is full of difficult decisions, traumatic events, and incidents that leave us with disempowering beliefs. But, with your intuition, you can override these codes and create magic. You can design a meaningful, purposeful, and fulfilling life.

Then there were times that I was not letting my intuition guide me. Times that I felt defeated, detached, and sorry for myself. These times I felt powerless, without any control to course correct.

In those times, being surrounded by loved ones who will speak up, tell the truth, and remind you to reclaim your power is critical.

I was so grateful when my friend, Jaime, heard me complaining and making excuses. I got a swift, loving kick in the butt when she said **No one is more masterful at manifesting than you! There's only one reason you do not have all the things you want in life yet. You are not being responsible for creating it.** Ouch! I needed that. Thank you for that truth bomb.

I experience the bliss of being in the flow-state of my genius when taking actions to access, activate, and align with my intuition. When I'm not, life becomes a struggle, full of stress, overwhelm, and effort. That is when I feel depressed and disempowered.

Sacred scripture that states *be still and know that I am God*.

When I make this my daily practice, I am attuned to my intuition. When I do this, I tap into the flow of being in the *right place* at the *right time*. Magically, I say precisely the *right things* to the *right people* that open up new doors, opportunities, and resources. The coincidences and unique encounters experienced throughout my life are so numerous I've lost count.

Also, there are equally as many experiences that I would love to blot out of my life and memory. By ignoring my intuition, I allowed a separation between the source of power and myself. These were the times when I lost myself.

Without a doubt, by not honoring my intuition, my life became unrecognizable. There was agony, despair, and grief. Knowing firsthand how dark and hopeless life can become, I am committed to supporting as many people as possible to regain their clarity, confidence, and courage.

Once you give yourself some grace and forgiveness to see your worth, value, and gifts, your power expands and multiplies exponentially. You tap into the flow-state and begin to feel fully supported!

As the genius Albert Einstein said, *the intuitive mind is a sacred gift, and the rational mind is a faithful servant. We have created a society that honors the servant and has forgotten the gift.*

My deepest desire for you is for you to remember the gift of intuition. Trust it absolutely because the world needs your genius right now!

Yvonne Larson

YVONNE LARSON

Yvonne Larson is a visionary catalyst, disruptor, and muse to entrepreneurs who are compelled to live a legacy life that has a massive positive impact in the world.

With numerous certifications in personal, professional, spiritual, and holistic therapies, many at the master practitioner level, and decades in private practice, she's uniquely positioned to design highly customized transformational tools for her clients.

Using these transformational tools, training, and mentorship she guides these leaders to thrive in their genius, and experience the real success metric, fulfillment.

She does this through the genius of her numerous talents, gifts, and intuition expressed through singing, speaking, and training that are delivered through my podcast, books, online courses, membership programs, mastermind, and JV partnerships.

Deeply passionate and committed to helping these experts move from the stress, overwhelm, and busy-ness of life in "survival mode" into the flow-state of living in their genius zone, she looks forward to helping you to crush it without compromising your joy. She invites you to reach out if you wish to connect or collaborate!

Scan the Code with your smartphone
to view a message from Yvonne Larson

ABOUT IMAN AGHAY

Compiler and Inspirer

Iman Aghay is a serial entrepreneur, international speaker, and 7-time #1 best-selling author.

He is best known as the founder of Success Road Academy and has created over 50 courses that help coaches, authors, speakers, and entrepreneurs grow their business aligned with their life purpose.

In 2010, Iman founded Success Road Academy, which has become an industry leader in online marketing and training. Through Success Road Academy, Iman has worked with over 150, 000 business owners, in various niches, and helped them expand their business and impact. Iman is also the founder of Entrepreneurs International Network, which has a community of over 150, 000 members in 5 countries. Iman is also part owner of JV Insider Circle, the world's leading community for entrepreneurs to find partnerships and deals, by utilizing community and connection. He continues making an impact through using community to connect entrepreneurs to their life purpose, and the people who can assist them.

He has become widely successful by helping other people to achieve greatness in their own lives.

Iman's TEDx talk is one of the world's top-rated speeches, which focuses on how to live a life with no regrets.

Iman has mastered creating a successful heart-centered business. He believes that all entrepreneurs can build a business based on their life's purpose. His vision of having a massive positive impact on 100 million people has fueled his love and passion for guiding entrepreneurs to success.

As the Leaders' Mentor, Iman's focus was and always is serving his clients and community with the utmost excellence and integrity.

Have you enjoyed the game-changing stories in this book?

We invite you to leave a review on Amazon, Goodreads or other online bookstores.

Be sure to check out the other books in this series:

Book 1
https://amzn.to/2GWjBAz

Book 2
https://amzn.to/3lH35mS

Book 3
https://amzn.to/3iSXDvv

Book 4
https://amzn.to/3lLNJOa

Book 5
https://amzn.to/3hqq0TS

Also, check out Iman's other books:
Ultimate Course Formula – How to Create and Sell Online Courses in 60 Days or Less
https://amzn.to/34NNzP6

Leaders Success Journal
https://amzn.to/2SOQth6

Made in the USA
Coppell, TX
03 November 2021

65148201R00115